THE COMPLETE
HUNTER™

BOWHUNTER'S
— GUIDE TO —
ACCURATE SHOOTING

Lon E. Lauber

Creative Publishing
international

Chanhassen, Minnesota

LON LAUBER has been an outdoor author for more than 20 years. His work has been published by National Geographic and Audubon, and most outdoor magazines including *Bow & Arrow, Bowhunter, Bowhunting World, Field and Stream, Outdoor Life, Petersen's Hunting* and *Sports Afield*. Lon is a 9-time Alaska State archery champion. He has bagged 41 official Pope and Young–class trophies. He lives in Spokane, Washington.

Creative Publishing international

Copyright © 2005 by Creative Publishing international, Inc.
18705 Lake Drive East
Chanhassen, MN 55317
1-800-328-3895
www.creativepub.com
All rights reserved.

President/CEO: Ken Fund
Vice President/Publisher: Linda Ball
Vice President/Retail Sales & Marketing: Kevin Haas
Executive Editor, Outdoor Group: Barbara Harold
Creative Director: Brad Springer
Project Manager: Tracy Stanley
Production Manager: Laura Hokkanen
Production Staff: Helga Thielen

Printed in China

10 9 8 7 6 5 4 3 2 1

DEDICATION

To my wonderful boys, Tyler and Trevor, who make me so proud.

And to all who love hunting with the bow and arrow—who are bent on making an accurate shot—and to the magnificent creatures we pursue that deserve our best effort to make a swift, humane kill.

ACKNOWLEDGMENTS

There have been many folks instrumental in my development as an archer and bowhunter. Without their passion, patience, guidance and support, I would not be the bowhunter I've become nor would this book be anywhere near this complete.

My deepest gratitude to my deceased father, Joe, and my oldest brother, best friend and confidant, Gary, for getting me started in archery. To Gary's wife, Kathie. To my sister, Nancy, and her husband, Hank, for being my most faithful cheerleaders throughout my photography and writing career. To my brother, Dale, his wife, Melinda (who is also the best office manager in the world), and their helpful daughter, Jessica, for always being there for me.

I would also like to thank Jim Velazquez, my original archery mentor and the man who initially encouraged me to pursue a career as a bowhunting writer and photographer. Jerry and Barb Fletcher of Fletcher's Archery in Wasilla, Alaska, and Josh Jones of Spokane Valley Archery for years of gracious support and being the best bow mechanics I know. Randy Ulmer, Bernie Pellerite, Fred Eichler and Josh Johnson for all the savvy advice. South Cox, Phil Lincoln, Bob Ameen, Harry Williamson, Mark Pfost, Sam Miller, Rich and Rob Eckles, Frank Jerik, Rick Forrest, Dan McKinley, Dave Murphy, Jim Cowgil, Jason Michael and others who are my hunting buddies and photo models, who do most of the work for which I get the credit. Bruce Friend and Gary Stevens of Skyline Sales, who believed in me and gave me the first chance at being a pro-staffer. Mathews and Browning Archery, Gold Tip Arrow Company, Rocky Mountain Broadheads, Easton Archery, Trophy Taker Arrow Rests, Sims Vibration Laboratory, Spot-Hogg Archery, Sonoran Bowhunting Products, Swarovski and Bushnell for their equipment and financial support; and, anyone else I may have overlooked, who over the years has lent me a helping hand or provided sage advice. Thank you so much!

BOWHUNTER'S GUIDE TO ACCURATE SHOOTING
by Lon E. Lauber

All Photographs Copyright © 2005 Lon E. Lauber

Library of Congress Cataloging-in-Publication Data
Lauber, Lon E.
    Bowhunter's guide to accurate shooting / Lon E. Lauber.
        p. cm.
    Includes an index.
    ISBN 1-58923-147-3 (hard cover)
    1. Bowhunting. I. Title.
SK36.L27 2005
799.2'15--dc22
                                    2004021163

BOWHUNTER'S GUIDE TO ACCURATE SHOOTING

CONTENTS

AUTHOR PREFACE 4

SECTION ONE: EQUIPMENT

CHAPTER 1
Bows: Components and Features 6

CHAPTER 2
Bowstrings: The Archer's Achilles' Heel 14

CHAPTER 3
Arrows: Consistent Flight 18

CHAPTER 4
Broadheads: Practical Advice 24

CHAPTER 5
Accessories: Just the Necessities 29

CHAPTER 6
Traditional Archery 34

SECTION TWO: PREPARATION

CHAPTER 7
Practicing Good Shooting Form 42

CHAPTER 8
Releasing the Arrow 50

CHAPTER 9
Understanding Bow Torque 58

CHAPTER 10
Preseason Shooting Preparation 62

CHAPTER 11
Estimating Yardage 66

CHAPTER 12
3-D Shooting 71

CHAPTER 13
Building Arrows 76

CHAPTER 14
Bow Tuning 82

SECTION THREE: PUTTING IT ALL TOGETHER

CHAPTER 15
Effective Shooting Range 92

CHAPTER 16
Balancing Accuracy and Arrow Speed 96

CHAPTER 17
The Mental Aspects of Bowhunting 102

CHAPTER 18
Shooting in Adverse Conditions 112

CHAPTER 19
Moment of Truth–Shooting Big Game 118

APPENDIX

Basement Bow Shop 124

Kinetic Energy Chart 125

Fitness for the Archer 125

Index 126

*W*ith ivory-tipped antlers glistening in the morning sun and warm breath steaming, an impressive white-tailed buck silently pads down the trail near your stand. For the first time all morning, you forget about the bone-chilling autumn weather. Adrenaline ripples though your veins like a nuclear-powered mouse. When the rut-crazed buck pauses in the mock scrape, you've already mentally tagged him and tasted his tenderloins. It feels like you've just won the lottery. Suddenly, however, the bow in your hand seems foreign; drawing it becomes a chore. Somehow you manage to pull back on the bowstring but your brain short-circuits when preparing to shoot. For some reason you flinch at the arrow's release. The broadhead-tipped projectile sails harmlessly over the buck's back and Mr. Big vanishes from your life like a puff of smoke in the wind.

This exasperating scenario happens all too often in the bowhunting woods. Mostly it's due to lack of preparation and insufficient knowledge. However, organization and hunting skills are not enough. You still have to "make the shot." That's the purpose of this book, to help you choose the right equipment and make the shot when it really counts. With forty years of archery experience and twenty-five exclusive years of bowhunting behind me, I know the natural high and elation of bringing a stalk to fruition. I also know that gut-wrenching ache when I've blundered at the moment of truth. It's the sweet satisfaction of success and the burning pit of failure in my stomach that has driven me to constantly improve my bowhunting and archery skills. I'd like to share with you what I've learned about shooting a bow accurately in a hunting situation.

The first thing you must understand and accept is it's one thing to stand in the backyard on a warm day and have your arrows thump a stationary bull's-eye shot after shot. It's quite another phenomenon to draw your bow undetected, aim at one hair of a live animal's chest and then execute flawless shooting form. This is especially true when you are cold and excited while leaning out of a tree stand or huffing and puffing after scurrying up a ridge to catch an elk crossing a mountain gully.

To be realistic, success shouldn't always be equated to killing. If harvesting an animal is your top priority, you shouldn't be hunting with a bow. Bowhunting is a low-percentage affair. You've made the choice to use a weapon that makes success more difficult. However, as ethical sportsmen and sportswomen, you owe it to the animals you hunt to be the most skilled and confident archer you can be. Furthermore, it's your duty to thoroughly know your equipment and have it set up properly. Choosing equipment and practicing the techniques illustrated in this book will dramatically improve your chances of becoming a consistently good shot with a bow in real-life hunting scenarios.

Good luck!

Lon

Longbow shooter Bill Morehead in the Nevada high country packing out his early-season mule deer buck.

CHAPTER ONE

Bows: Components and Features

After fourteen days of thigh-burning, lung-busting ascents in pursuit of a trophy Dall ram, I finally got my chance. Cautiously, I crept to the mountain's edge and peeked over. There they were; seven white monarchs feeding and milling their way to a cliff-side bedding area. My laser range finder measured 59 yards (54 m) to the biggest of the bunch.

A quick scan of the scene and my experience told me to aim with the 50-yard (45.5-m) pin to compensate for the downhill angle. Slowly, I drew my bow, concentrating on an imaginary quarter-size spot behind his shoulder, and released. The arrow arched down the hill and flicked through the ram within inches of where I was aiming!

The author with a Pope and Young–class Dall ram he shot at 59 yards in the Alaska Range Mountains.

Looking back at that success, I realize that other than my persistence, tagging that ram was due to a forgiving and, thus, accurate hunting bow.

All bows are inherently accurate—as long as nothing mechanical changes, such as the string elongating, limbs shifting in limb pockets, bolts backing out, etc. Even an untuned bow can shoot a broadhead-tipped arrow to the same point of impact, shot after shot when launched from a machine in a laboratory environment. Most of us, however, don't shoot with machine consistency nor do we hunt in a wind- and temperature-controlled climate. Thus, choosing and setting up archery tackle for optimum "forgiveness" and learning to shoot with repeatable form are the keys to accurate shooting.

What constitutes a forgiving hunting bow is a personal concept that ultimately only you can decide. There are, however, certain features you should look for when choosing a hunting bow. In my opinion, accurate shooting is priority one.

Regardless of whether you prefer a longbow, recurve or compound bow, the forgiving hunting bow should have the following five traits:

• It should be fairly simple.

• It must have the correct draw length, draw weight and let-off for you.

• A hunting bow should balance well in your hand and feel comfortable from a weight standpoint.

• The brace height and overall length of a hunting bow should be conducive to accurate shooting.

• And it should be quiet when shot—any noise more than a dull "thunk" is unacceptable.

Bowhunter Sam Miller at full draw, showing relaxed bow hand and good form.

Keep It Simple, Stupid

The old adage, "Keep it simple, Stupid," is spot-on when it comes to a hunting bow. Simple is just better. There's less to go wrong. At crunch time, a Star Wars–type bow with too many gizmos is counterproductive. Also, a complicated bowhunting rig is a nightmare to repair in the field.

Whether you prefer a longbow, recurve or compound bow depends on your hunting skills, the time you have to practice and which type you can shoot best. Longbows and recurves are pleasing to the eye and the epitome of simple—a bow and a string. They are lightweight, easy to maneuver when hunting, shoot quietly and are incredibly deadly in the hands of a well-practiced archer. Non-compound bows are quick-shooting tools. They are ideal for snap-shooting or instinctive aiming styles. "Stick bows" get the nod in certain hunting scenarios. For instance, while hunting flying birds or fish, a recurve is the ticket. If your target animal will always be close, like a bear on bait or whitetails from a tree stand, a recurve would be an excellent choice.

However, I do feel recurves and longbows are for expert bowhunters—not the novice. Any non-compound bow requires extensive practice to tone muscles and keep the shooting eye sharp. It's sort of like using a .410 shotgun for bird hunting. It certainly works but you'd better be a crack shot who's more concerned with the spirit of the hunt than with harvesting game.

If practice time is limited due to the reality of life and you'll be hunting game beyond 25 yards (22 m), a compound bow is a better choice. The average archer can shoot "hunting accurate" with a properly fitted, well-tuned compound bow with minimal practice. This doesn't mean if you choose to hunt with a compound bow, you don't have to practice. With let-off, bow sights and a release, the compound bow is easier to shoot consistently.

If you choose to hunt with a stick bow, a good place to start is a bow about 60 inches (150 cm) long or longer with a peak draw weight of 40 to 60 pounds (18 to 27 kg). Of course, your ultimate choice depends on state law, your physical strength and what game animals you intend to pursue. (Chapter 6 goes into more detail on shooting traditional bows.)

While it's true a compound bow is more complicated than a stick bow, it can be set up judiciously. I've hunted with simple compound bow rigs in the wilderness for years and they've performed very well for me. There are simply more variables when choosing a compound bow.

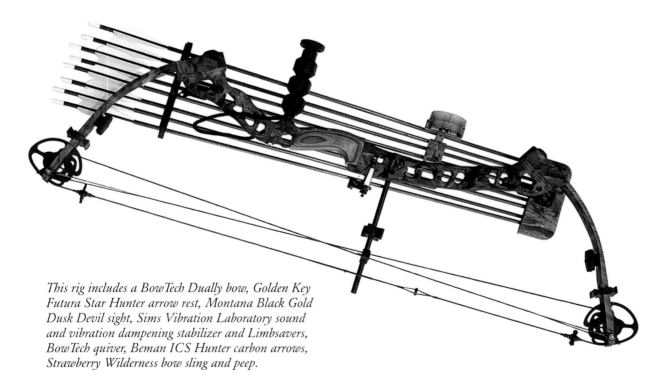

This rig includes a BowTech Dually bow, Golden Key Futura Star Hunter arrow rest, Montana Black Gold Dusk Devil sight, Sims Vibration Laboratory sound and vibration dampening stabilizer and Limbsavers, BowTech quiver, Beman ICS Hunter carbon arrows, Strawberry Wilderness bow sling and peep.

Draw Length

Without exception, draw length is the most important aspect of shooting any bow accurately.

Too short of a draw length forces you to scrunch up, making it difficult to relax and shoot with consistently good form. Also, too short of a draw length unnecessarily robs arrow speed and penetration. Conversely, a bow that's too long causes overextension. Leaning back with your torso and stretching your arms to keep the bow taut makes relaxing and follow-through nearly impossible. A bow that's too long in draw will slap the shooter's arm with the bowstring or the string will catch on bulky hunting clothes, throwing the arrow off target.

In my opinion, too long of a draw length is the number one malady of bowhunters today. I'd say about 85 percent of bowhunters would shoot more accurately if they shortened their draw length by 1 inch (2.5 cm) or more. It seems everyone is so caught up in arrow speed they forget about the importance of accurate shooting. An extra inch of draw length may produce an additional 10 feet (3 m) per second (fps/mps) in arrow speed but if it comes at the cost of inconsistent shot placement, it's not worth it.

Of the two, shooting a little bit short and bending at the elbow of the bow arm is a better choice.

The best way to check for proper draw length is to get professional help from a knowledgeable archery technician at a pro shop. He or she will help you with correct form. They'll use a lightweight recurve with a measuring arrow to determine your proper draw length. Be sure to check your draw length with the release aid or finger tab and the shooting form anchor point you intend to use while hunting. A beginner should select a bow with variable draw length slots. Initially set up the bow in the middle of the draw length choice. This gives you leeway when your form, anchor point or style of releasing the arrow changes.

The easiest way to check your draw length at home is to place one end of a yardstick (meter stick) against the top of your sternum (bottom of your throat) and reach out to the front with both hands. Clasp the stick with flattened fingers. The distance to the end of your middle fingers will be close to your proper draw length. When I check my draw length this way, it shows 26 1/2 inches (67.3 cm). I shoot a 26-inch-draw-length (66-cm) bow but we are all built differently. Some people have long arms in comparison to their torso; others may have short arms but long hands. Thus, proper draw length is as individual as we are.

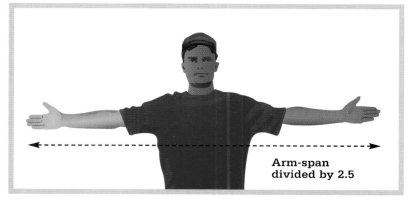

Arm-span divided by 2.5

To measure your draw length, determine the length of your arm-span in inches. Stand with your hands out and palms facing forward. Don't stretch when measuring—just stand naturally. Have someone else help you, and measure from the tip of one middle finger to the other. Then simply divide that number by 2.5. The quotient is your approximate draw length (in inches) for your body size.

Getting professional help to determine your proper draw length is a crucial preliminary step in building a solid foundation of good shooting form. Here, Jessica Lauber is being measured for proper draw length by Spokane Valley Archery's Josh Jones.

Draw Weight and Let-Off

Careful consideration must be employed when choosing the draw weight and percentage of let-off of a compound bow. These two factors, in part, dictate how fast your arrow flies, can alter the arrow's penetration and affect your ability to shoot accurately.

From a hunter's perspective, being able to draw your bow in slow motion with no exaggerated gyrations when you are cold and excited is the maximum draw weight you should consider. Normally this is at least 5 to 10 pounds (2.25 to 4.5 kg) less than you could shoot on a warm day while practicing in the backyard. Try sitting on the living room floor, legs extended in front of you. Now draw your bow without having to give it the heave-ho. Using this "not when hunting" drill is a way to determine appropriate draw weight.

I botched a shot opportunity at a trophy whitetail in Manitoba because of too much draw weight. I had backed off the poundage from my normal 70 pounds (31.5 kg) to 65 (29.25 kg), figuring the lighter draw weight would be a sufficient reduction to pull the bow even when cold and excited. I was wrong. After six days of ten-hour vigils, a dandy buck walked within 16 yards (14.5 m) of my tree stand, turned broadside and looked away. I couldn't have choreographed a better scenario! With the excitement, self-induced

pressure to score on the last evening and the cold, I couldn't draw my bow! Finally, I thrust the bow in the air and yanked with all my might. I got the bow to full draw but the buck bolted from the excess movement.

It's a real balancing act to select enough draw weight to achieve relatively flat arrow trajectory and still be able to shoot accurately. Frequently I try different arrows and different draw weights to determine the most potent setup—that I can shoot accurately. When I start pulling more than 70 pounds (31.5 kg) or shooting arrows lighter than 350 grains (22.68 g), my group size enlarges to where the extra arrow speed is not worth the loss of accuracy. Shooting too much draw weight makes one shake more, destabilizing the sight picture. It's much better to maintain accuracy with a slower, heavier arrow than to miss or, worse, make a bad hit with a light, fast arrow. With the aid of a laser range finder, a slower, more arching arrow isn't the handicap it was just a few years ago.

Conversely, you must shoot enough draw weight to be legal in your hunting area and have the rig produce enough kinetic energy to kill your target animal in a humane fashion.

When choosing a hunting bow, consider quarry size and realistically determine your physical capabilities to draw a bow under pressure and still shoot straight. Luckily most modern compound bows are designed with about a 10-pound-draw-weight (4.5-kg) adjustment range. You can start out low and work your way up as muscles tone.

Also consider how much let-off from the bow's peak weight is best for you. Most of today's bows offer either/both 65 or 80 percent let-off settings. Initially, more let-off would seem logical; the bow would be easier to hold at full draw. However, some state laws have 65-percent-maximum let-off restrictions. Most tournament archers prefer more holding weight because it gives them a cleaner release. All else being equal, a bow with 65 percent let-off will shoot the arrow slightly faster than the same setup with 80 percent let-off.

The only major benefit to shooting a bow with 80 percent let-off is for a whitetail hunter to draw prematurely, hold at full draw for a minute or two and be ready when a buck walks into a clear shooting lane.

Here, South Cox holds at full draw, waiting for this Sitka blacktail to stop and offer an ethical shot.

Brace Height

Brace height is the perpendicular distance from the string to the pivot point of the bow's handle. That pivot point is the most recessed part of the bow handle and is usually directly below the hole drilled for the arrow rest.

Brace height affects arrow speed and accuracy. The shorter the brace height, the farther the string travels forward upon launch. This longer power stroke increases arrow velocity. The fastest bows have brace heights as short as 5 inches (12.7 cm). For the average bowhunter, however, any bow with a brace height of 6½ inches (16.5 cm) or less becomes more critical to shooting accurately. Bows with a short brace height are more critical and less forgiving of shooting-form errors because of more severe angles. Since there is little distance between the arrow nock and the pivot point of the bow upon arrow launch, the slightest hand torque will send arrows off target. Also, bows with a short brace height are notorious for causing string slap against the arm.

I prefer 7 or 8 inches (17.8 or 20.3 cm) of brace height on my hunting bows. I want my rig to be forgiving of my human errors and still cast the arrow close to where I'm aiming.

Brace height is a crucial consideration when choosing a forgiving bow for hunting. A short-brace-height bow, say less than 7 inches, is more critical to shoot accurately, similar to shooting a short-barreled handgun.

Axle-to-Axle Length

The overall length of the bow affects accuracy and the ability to maneuver the bow in hunting situations. The shorter the bow, the more severe the string angle at full draw. Also, a longer draw length causes a more severe string angle. With a 26-inch (66-cm) draw I can shoot a shorter bow and not get the steep string angle a person with a 30-inch (76-cm) draw would have while using the same bow.

That steep string angle affects accuracy much as a short brace height does. Any little variance in the bow arm/hand will send the arrow off target. A severe string angle causes finger pinch for those who shoot with a tab. This makes shooting uncomfortable and releasing the arrow cleanly more difficult. Steeper string angles are more likely to nip the arrow off the string at full draw. There's nothing more frustrating than coming to full draw from an awkward hunting stance only to have the arrow get pinched off the string and clank on the ground.

Axle-to-axle length is not as important to accuracy as is brace height. This is especially true of bows in the 30- to 35-inch (76- to 89-cm) range employing a large cam and idler wheel. These bows draw and shoot similar to a much longer bow.

Consider your hunting needs when deciding axle-to-axle length. Do you hunt from tree stands or a ground blind with limited maneuverability where a short bow would be beneficial? I've had the best luck with bows in the 34- to 40-inch (86.4- to 101.6-cm) length for shooting with a release aid. When I shot with fingers, I preferred bows with an even longer axle-to-axle length.

Overall length of a compound bow combined with draw length determines string angle at full draw. A steeper string angle usually equates to a less-accurate hunting rig.

Bow Weight

It's a matter of simple physics: It takes more inertia to move a heavier bow off target. A light bow will move around more in the wind and exaggerate the inevitable human wobble involved in archery. That's why long-range marksmen use rifles with "bull" barrels—the heavier barrel stays on target better. Also, a lightweight bow will "jump" more upon arrow launch, much like a lighter rifle produces more recoil than a heavier gun.

On the other hand, you don't want to lug around a boat anchor for a bow! Your choice depends on your physical strength and the type of hunting you do. If you use an ATV to access a tree stand, consider a heavier bow. If you intend to backpack 15 miles (24 km) into elk country, a lighter bow is the way to go. Remember, the actual bow weight is only about 65 percent of the final product; sights, arrows, quiver and a stabilizer all add to it. The overall weight of the bow rig should not cause undue stress when holding the bow out in front of you.

Silence Is Golden

A quiet-shooting bow may not help you shoot with more accuracy but it will definitely help you successfully harvest game. Sound travels at 1,100 fps (335 mps). Even with an arrow launched at 300 fps (91 mps), the sound of the shot is reaching the target animal about 3.66 times faster than the arrow. If your hunting rig produces arrow speeds of about 250 fps (76 mps), the sound of the bow going off will reach a deer's ears 4.4 times faster than the

arrow! The bottom line in bowhunting is the sound of shooting will always get to your intended quarry before the arrow. Thus, it is critical to do everything you can to achieve a quiet-shooting bow.

Here are some suggestions:

• During a laboratory test, I discovered the majority of bow noise and vibration comes from the bowstring and limbs, not the riser. So, string silencers and limb vibration-dampening devices are prudent investments.

• Shoot a bow with a higher brace, heavier arrow, less draw weight and fewer accessories.

• If using a bow-mounted quiver, make certain the broadhead hood is well insulated and the arrow clip is as far down the shafts and as close to the fletching as possible. A short quiver allows the arrows to vibrate terribly when shooting.

• Add a vibration-dampening stabilizer.

• Make sure your arrow rest doesn't clank during the shot cycle. Adhesive-backed fleece works well to absorb sound from the arrow rest and sight-window portion of the riser.

With so many brands, makes and models available these days, it's hard to select a hunting bow. If you make accurate shooting your top priority, your choices narrow to what's really important. A good hunting bow should be simple, of proper draw length, draw weight and let-off and have around 7 inches (17.8 cm) of brace height. Make it quiet and as long and heavy as possible for your hunting style. Finally, a bow that instills confidence by looking, feeling and shooting well for you, is the best one—regardless of brand name.

CHAPTER TWO

Bowstrings: The Archer's Achilles' Heel

My breath smoked in the autumn brisk-ness as I rock-hopped along a milky, glacier-fed river in the mighty Alaska Range Mountains. Instead of watching my step, my thoughts drifted off to visions of tall-racked caribou floating over the fiery-colored tundra. An electric tin-gle of anticipation rippled up my spine. I was in bowhunting heaven. Just then I slipped on slimy stones and down I went. My bow's string exploded when it slammed into sharp rocks!

As I picked up my powerless bow and brushed the grit off my bruised hands and knees, the thought went through my head, "The Achilles' heel of a bow

is definitely the string!" Even though I was more than 100 air miles (160 km) from the nearest archery pro shop, I wasn't completely distraught. I was well aware that a bow's string is its weak link. I had come prepared on this wilderness hunt.

I remember anxiously racing against the setting sun to re-string and re-sight-in my bow. With the help of a BowMaster portable bow press and an extra, pre-shot string, I had my bow shooting again in about 15 minutes. Just before dark, I was grouping prac-tice broadheads into a muddy riverbank. The next evening, after a 10-hour stalk, I arrowed a dandy, Pope and Young–class caribou.

Can you imagine what a disaster that hunt would have been if I hadn't been prepared? It doesn't have to be an expensive wilderness adventure to have a damaged or broken bowstring ruin a hunt.

The Basics

A bowstring has two main purposes. The first is to transfer energy from your arms and back muscles to the limbs of the bow. The second is to transfer that stored energy from the bow into the arrow. This thrust propels the arrow and gives it a direction in which to fly. In short, a bowstring does the same thing as a tennis racket, Ping-Pong paddle or golf club—it acts as a catalyst to reassign energy. And, like any of these other sport tools, a bowstring must transfer energy efficiently, in a nearly identical manner and for months or years to come. If the string doesn't meet these criteria, it's going to make shooting accurately nearly impossible.

Luckily for us, today's bowstrings easily meet these basic requirements. The downside is there are so many string choices, it gets confusing as to which brand or high-tech material to choose. Here is some information that will make you more aware of just how important your bowstring is.

String Terminology

With regard to bowstring terminology, there are two concepts that are frequently misused or incorrectly used. The first is "stretch." The proper and accurate definition of stretch, in our case, is the temporary or recoverable elongation of the string caused by the dynamic tension of the bow. This is similar to what happens to your arm during a vigorous handshake, or pulling on a rubber band.

The second term, "creep," is the continual and permanent elongation of the string caused by the load or tension from the bow limbs. This is akin to being hooked up to a torture rack with your arms and legs being pulled in opposite directions for months.

So in this chapter, I will use the proper definitions to avoid confusion—in spite of what terms some manufacturers use. Remember, with most string

materials it takes about 200 shots for the material to creep into the manufacturers' specified length. So shoot your bow quite a bit before doing your ultimate, fine-tuning.

Other basic terms include "serving," which is a horizontal wrap of string material that covers and protects the linear strands of a bowstring at points of excessive wear. "Nock set" is either a brass clip, some string material knotted around the string, or the position of a D-loop at the precise and repeatable point where you nock the arrow.

Nock Fit

The proper fit or tension between the bowstring and the arrow's nock is crucial to consistent accuracy and practical hunting situations. Most "experts" claim a good compromise would be a snug fit where the arrow's nock snaps onto the string yet loose enough so it can be pulled off the string with a slight, two-fingered tug. A loose-fitting nock will increase arrow speed a little but if the nock is too loose, the arrow may fall off the string when drawing or cause a dry fire. A tight nock is noisier when nocking an arrow in a hunting situation and it can cause inconsistent arrow groups from poor arrow flight. About the only thing a super-tight nock fit helps with is discovering a cracked nock.

If you get serious about customizing your bow's string (using fewer strands of a stronger material for faster arrow flight), be sure your nock fit is good. The easiest way is to re-serve the string with a material of such diameter to give you a good nock-to-string fit. You should have at least 3 inches (7.6 cm) of serving above your nock set to ensure that the upward pressure of your release or fingers does not make the serving slip.

Custom Strings

Because a bow's string truly is its weak point, many top tournament archers and bowhunters now use custom-made strings. The best ones I've found are Mathews Zebra Twist strings and Winner's Choice custom strings. Other manufacturers have comparable strings, which may work well for you.

The patented Zebra ZS Twist strings use counter-clockwise (Z) and clockwise (S) twisted filaments bundled together to make a complete string. This balances the string to dramatically reduce peep rotation. Also, the two-color design makes it easier to separate the strands for peep installation.

Mathews' other custom string is called Tiger Twist. This string is manufactured with the same patented ZS twist but employs different materials. This string has virtually no creep so your bow is unlikely to come out of tune due to the permanent elongation of the string. All else being equal, a Tiger Twist string will slow your arrow down about 3 to 4 fps (0.9 to 1.2 mps). As with most things, there are trade-offs. Do you want a faster-shooting string that elongates more over its life or a slightly slower shooting string that doesn't creep? Only you can decide.

Another source of excellent custom-made strings is Winner's Choice. Their strings and cables are constructed with a unique process that pre-elongates the string fibers so your string and cables stay at the desired length for the entire useful life of the product. Winner's Choice also has a patented method for serving strings that virtually eliminates serving separations. Their serving material has a slick surface ideal for finger shooters.

One other addition to Winner's Choice products is a short length of cord placed through the exact center of the bowstring before it is pre-twisted. This divider makes peep installation in the proper place a snap. I have Winner's Choice strings installed on all my compound bows.

String Care

Most string problems are caused by a bowhunter's negligence or ignorance. When hunting, carry your bow with the riser down so if you do slip, the first part of the bow to contact the ground is the riser—not the string. I switch off between carrying my bow by the handle, then the bus cables and the string. This way my hand doesn't get too tired nor do I wear out the strings. Nowadays, there are several bow slings to disperse the bow's weight over your shoulder and protect the string/cable with a casing material. APA Ultimate makes a slick little bow-carrying handle that comes with a rubber "O" ring. Thread the "O" ring through your belt; then you can quickly hang the bow from the "O" ring. This frees up both hands for glassing or other two-handed chores. Also, when winching your bow up and down from a tree stand, connect the pull rope to the top wheel or bow limb and not the string.

One common problem is too tightly crimping-on brass nock sets. This destroys the serving and, regardless of phenomenal linear strength, most modern string materials don't take crimping too well. I've found it's much better to tie on a nock set with #4 braided nylon serving material or Fast Flight than to use brass nocks. There are several advantages: One, its lighter weight; you may gain a few feet (meters) per second in arrow velocity. Two, it doesn't slip like brass and it won't cut the serving or crush the individual string strands from jagged edges inside a brass nock. This preserves string life and strength. And three, a tied-in nock set can be replaced in the field without nock pliers.

Remember, though, when tying-in a nock set, it's better to clip and glue the knot ends than burn them. All the new string materials have relatively low melting points. Thus, burning can weaken or destroy string fibers. If you insist on burning knot ends, be sure the heat rises beside the string instead of under it. You may want to consider products like Brownell's Liquid Lok to prevent serving ends from unraveling and reducing wear on servings.

Here are a few other string maladies to avoid:

• String slap on your bow arm will wear out a string faster than anything. Learn proper shooting form so you never have the string slapping your arm. If it does, you may be shooting too long of a draw length, gripping the bow handle incorrectly or standing at an improper angle to the target. Remember, for a right-handed shooter, a low left shoulder, slightly bent elbow and a slightly open stance (chest facing more toward the target) will increase the angle between your bow arm and the string.

• Don't place your bottom wheel or cam directly on the ground. When you do, the string and wax pick up debris that eventually acts like sandpaper and causes unnecessary wear.

• Never install a peep sight or other string accessory under full tension. Be sure to use a bow press to relax string tension for these chores. If you don't, minute fibers or individual strands may break or be damaged.

• Use a string loop to reduce the wear on the string from a mechanical release. The release is attached to the loop and doesn't ever touch the string, thus preserving string and serving life. However, for small-stature archers who don't want to lose any more draw length or arrow speed by using a loop, tie one layer of Fast Flight serving material right below the nock set. This extra layer saves the serving from direct contact with the release aid and it's easy to replace in the field if necessary.

• Waxing the string regularly is the best preventive maintenance. Each fray is actually a miniature strand breaking. There are many kinds of string wax available—including beeswax and synthetics. There are even unscented formulas.

Regularly waxing a bowstring (inset) will extend string life and reduce fraying as seen on this well-worn example.

THE D-LOOP

The D-loop is perhaps the single most effetive way to improve accuracy (for those using a release aid and compound bow). Here are two reasons: The arrow is positioned between the loop knots. The release is attached to the center of the "D" and not below the arrow like a direct string hookup. This puts all of the bow's forward thrust directly behind the nock/arrow. It translates into cleaner arrow flight, easier tuning and improved broadhead flight.

A string loop eliminates release-to-string wear and greatly reduces any twist or torque on the string caused by the tension of the release and drawing the bow. This lengthens string life and improves consistent launch and arrow flight. When tree stand hunting and stalking, there are times you may have to draw and let down several times before finally making the shot. The string D-loop allows this without having to re-nock the arrow as you would with a traditional hook up.

Along these same lines, a D-loop eliminates the release pinching the nock off the string when shooting at steep angles. A properly installed D-loop will automatically align your peep sight, thus eliminating the need for peep tubing. And, with effort, you can twist a D-loop up or down the string to change nock height when tuning.

About the only draw-  backs to using a string loop are that you'll lose about ½ inch (1 cm) of effective draw length, and it can be frustrating to tie on (until you get the hang of it).

There are three basic options in the world of D-loops. One, tie in the loop yourself or have a qualified clerk at your local pro shop do it. Two, use metal D-loops available from Quality Archery Designs. Its Ultra-Nok is clamped onto the bowstring and secured with tiny screws. Three, get a pre-fabricated loop made by Rock-It Outdoors. This loop has center serving just like a bowstring so it maintains its D shape and lasts a long time. You do have to remove your bowstring to install this one, however.

CHAPTER THREE

Arrows: Consistent Flight

On the first evening of a blacktail hunt in Northern California I shot a brand-new broadhead-tipped practice arrow at a McKenzie 3-D deer target from 60 yards (55 m). When the arrow hit about 16 inches (41 cm) high and to the right from what I thought was a well-executed shot, my confidence was shaken.

Just prior to the hunt, I'd been conducting some accuracy evaluations with three styles of fletching. The ones I'd chosen for the hunt had produced three-arrow groups averaging 4.3 inches (10.9 cm) at 60 yards (55 m)—with fixed-blade broadheads. I hadn't shot a "flier" in weeks. I shot the same arrow four times; each shot impacted high/right. Confused, I grabbed two more practice arrows and proceeded to thump the 10-ring six times in a row. My confidence was returning but I knew there was a problem with that particular arrow.

After the hunt, with the aid of a shooting machine, I determined the arrow had poor nock alignment. A few days later, with my returned confidence, I killed a blacktail at 63 yards (57 m).

I learned a good lesson: If you haven't shot a particular arrow before, how do you know it will fly true? You don't. So I even go so far as re-sharpening or replacing blades on practice broadheads to ensure consistent-flying hunting arrows.

Without consistent-flying arrows, bowhunting accuracy and, ultimately, the humane harvest of game would be like winning the lottery—nothing but a chance. You owe it to the big game you hunt to put thought, effort and financial investment into this important component of a bowhunting rig.

Whether aluminum or carbon, feathers or vanes, several factors come into play to make accurate hunting arrows:

• Consistently straight and aligned nocks, shafts and broadheads for concentricity.

• Consistent spine so each arrow flexes the same with every shot.

• Sufficient fletching at the rear of the arrow to provide steerage of the broadhead-tipped shaft.

• The front-of-center (FOC) or balance point of the arrow should be 8 to 15 percent tip-heavy.

• Consistent weight.

• Consistent length.

Bowhunter Jim Posekany at full draw, western Oregon.

Left, Lon with a black bear taken near Valdez, Alaska, with an Easton 2213 aluminum arrow. Right, Harry Williamson with a Pope and Young–class whitetail buck taken near Spokane, Washington, with a Beman ICS Hunter carbon arrow.

Straightness

Crooked arrows cause projectile wobble. Any wobble will cause the surface area of the broadhead blades to catch wind. If enough air drags across the broadhead, the front end of the arrow starts competing with the fletching for control and the arrow planes off course. Furthermore, a wobbling broadhead-tipped arrow lucky enough to hit the target animal will do so with greatly reduced penetration. All of the arrow's weight and velocity should be directly behind the broadhead for ultimate penetration. Finally, when arrows don't group well, confidence deteriorates. If you think you're going to miss, you probably will.

Spine

Like straightness, the spine or stiffness of the arrow should be consistent from shaft to shaft. Upon launch of the arrow, all of the bow's thrust is channeled into the nock end of the arrow. It takes momentum to get the broadhead moving. At this point, the arrow flexes as it's darting out of the bow. This is called paradox.

The trick is to match the arrow's spine to the draw weight and draw length to get just the right amount of paradox. If the arrow acts too weak in spine, wobbling inconsistent arrow flight occurs. Conversely, selecting an arrow substantially too stiff in spine will net the same results. When using an arrow selection chart to get in the ballpark of what arrow spine you need, it's better to err toward stiffness. With broadheads, slightly over-spined arrows will group better than under-spined arrows.

The spine of aluminum arrows is indicated with a four-digit code, 2213 for example. The 22 stands for $^{22}/_{64}$ inch (8.7 mm) in diameter. The 13 indicates .013 inch (0.3 mm) of arrow wall thickness. It's the shaft diameter that mostly affects arrow spine, whereas wall thickness mostly affects arrow weight.

The spine designator of carbon arrows is similar. Some sort of numbering system is used. For example, Gold Tip arrows marked 5575 are spined to be shot from a bow with a draw weight between 55 and 75 pounds (25 and 34 kg). A Beman ICS carbon arrow spine is marketed by spine deflection, such as 340, 400, 500. The higher the number means the arrow flexes more or acts weaker in spine. You will find each brand of carbon arrow has its own spine indication numbers.

Fletching

Whether made of plastic vanes or feathers, the fletching's job is twofold. Its first duty is to cause air-surface drag, thus giving the arrow stability and maintain direction in flight. Its second chore is spinning the arrow. Gluing fletches on the shaft with a slightly offset or helical angle spins the arrow. It's the same concept as riflings in a gun barrel. It makes the projectile fly straighter and more consistent.

Three fletches set 120 degrees apart is standard, but some archers use four fletches positioned 90 degrees apart. Regardless of preference, the shape, size and helical of fletching compared to the amount of broadhead blade surface area determines how well the fletching will control the arrow. Too small of fletch for the broadhead makes unstable arrow flight. Too much fletch and velocity is squandered.

Front-of-Center

By choice, cavemen hurled spears consisting of a heavy rock tied to the front of a long stick. That projectile certainly flew in a point-heavy manner. You can bet those early humans tried every combination to get the most accurately flying weapon. Their lives depended on it. We may be slightly more sophisticated but the principle is the same.

An arrow's front-of-center (FOC) or balance point is crucial to consistent and, thus, accurate flight.

ARROW SPINE

End view of an aluminum arrow

.013" Wall Thickness

Shaft Diameter: $^{22}/_{64}$"

This example shows the cross section of an Easton arrow 2213. The shaft diameter is $^{22}/_{64}$" and the wall thickness is .013". Easton aluminum arrow numbering system indicates shaft diameter in 64th's of an inch with the first two digits (22). The third and fourth digits indicate arrow wall thickness in thousandths of an inch (13).

Many studies have indicated broadhead-tipped arrows group best when they are between 8 and 15 percent nose-heavy. Increasing broadhead/insert weight increases the percentage of FOC. Using lighter fletching will do the same thing; heavier, the opposite.

I've experimented extensively with FOC and its effects on my broadhead groups. I usually end up shooting arrows with about 10 to 12 percent FOC. More than that, trajectory increases at long range. This causes my pin gap to expand (in other words, I have to judge yardage more accurately). Going much lighter than 8 percent seems to open up my group size when shooting broadheads.

Experiment with different weight broadheads and fletching styles. Go with the combination that shoots most accurately.

Weight

Arrow weight is indicated in grains. For reference, 437.5 grains (28.35 g) equals 1 ounce. Variances of more than 15 grains (0.97 g) will affect your group sizes significantly. I doubt most archers could see the difference in a 10-grain (0.65-g) disparity except at long range. However, from a confidence perspective, I like my arrows to weigh within 2 grains (0.13 g) of each other.

I have an electronic grain scale to weigh each arrow and broadhead. Just because the package says 125-grain (8.10-g) broadheads, however, doesn't mean they all are exactly the same weight. This is a "ballpark" figure. It's always a good idea to check your components for consistent weight. Put a slightly heavier broadhead on a lighter shaft. With some shuffling, getting nine or ten "matched-weight" broadhead-tipped arrows out of a dozen is possible.

Length

All else being equal, a shorter arrow will act stiffer in spine. You already know selecting the proper arrow spine is paramount to accurate shooting. Cut all arrows the same length and don't mix arrow types/spines. In general, a longer arrow is a more stable projectile than a shorter one. From a

hunting standpoint, however, any arrow between 25 inches (63.5 cm) and 32 inches (81.3 cm) that is properly fletched with sufficient FOC will fly well. Remember, consistency is the name of the accuracy game.

Carbon Versus Aluminum

Some archers still use wood arrows. Most hunters, nowadays, choose aluminum, but carbon arrows are rapidly gaining market share. I've extensively shot arrows made of both materials. It's all about shot placement. I've never shot an animal I believe would have expired quicker using one material over the other. Success comes from confidence in equipment and your shooting skills.

There are pros and cons associated with both materials. Here are some positive characteristics to take into account when choosing arrow shaft material:

• Carbon arrows are extremely durable. They can usually withstand other arrows smacking against them and take a glancing blow from a rock or tree. But point-on impact with a hard surface usually makes them splinter in banana-peel fashion. While stump shooting on a hunt, I can usually use the same two arrows all week with no ill effects. When I shoot aluminum, the same stump shooting might destroy several arrows in the process.

• Carbon's lighter weight-to-spine ratio allows shooting a lighter arrow with more draw weight for increased velocity and flatter trajectory.

• The narrow diameter of carbon arrows makes them less affected by wind.

Carbon arrows are durable and have a light weight-to-spine ratio that helps with flatter trajectory.

• The skinny carbon shafts have less surface area and tend to penetrate slightly better than aluminum.

There are, however, some drawbacks to carbon arrows, which include:

• They are more expensive.

• The skinny shafts don't leave much space between fletches for arrow-rest clearance.

• The narrow shaft inhibits the amount of helical ("twist") you can put on the fletching.

• Lining up broadheads with fletching must be done at the time of gluing inserts. Once the epoxy sets, it's difficult and time consuming to remove or rotate an insert.

• Carbon arrows can't be straightened. You are stuck with however straight or crooked they come from the factory.

For the past seven years I've used carbon arrows for hunting with stellar results. Overall, a quality carbon arrow is an excellent choice for hunting.

The reasons aluminum arrows are so popular include the following:

• They are reasonably priced.

• Standard sizes can be found just about anywhere.

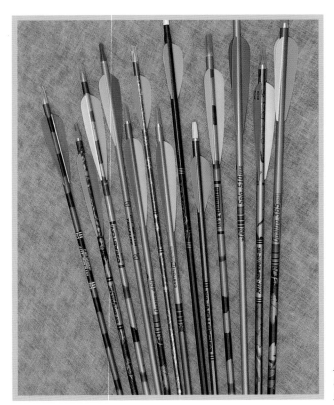

Aluminum arrows have long been the staple for bowhunting and are still a viable choice.

• They are easy to fletch.

• The hot-melt glue allows you to reheat and rotate inserts/broadheads easily for better concentricity and alignment with fletching.

• The larger diameter allows more helical on fletches.

• Vane clearance on the arrow rest with fat shafts is a snap.

• There are usually at least three different weight arrows for any given spine. With so many choices, you can fine-tune your rig for perfect flight and have some latitude regarding trajectory and kinetic energy.

• Aluminum arrows can be "recycled" with a little finesse and an arrow straightener.

The drawbacks to aluminum arrows are few:

• They tend to break and bend beyond repair more easily than carbon.

• The larger surface area of aluminum shafts catch slightly more wind and may impede penetration slightly.

Don't overlook Easton's aluminum/carbon composite (ACC) arrows. They are hybrid arrows, combining a carbon wrap with an aluminum tube. They have most all the benefits of both materials and very few drawbacks. Easton ACC shafts are one of the most accurate arrow shafts I've ever used.

I've probably killed 80 percent of my big game with aluminum arrows. Not one animal noticed I wasn't using fancy carbon arrows. Like most aspects of archery, arrow shaft material is a personal choice.

Feathers Versus Vanes

With something gained there's always something lost, and so it goes with feather fletching or plastic vanes. I've hunted with both and appreciate them for their individual qualities and sometimes curse them for their drawbacks.

Feathers

Feathers are considerably lighter than vanes. Thus, all else being equivalent, feather-fletched arrows exit the bow with more velocity. However, that same lighter arrow loses downrange velocity faster than the heavier arrow with vanes. For example, if you shot two identical arrows (except for the fletching material) at the same time, the arrow with feathers would win the "race" out to about 40 yards. From 40 to 80 yards (36.4 to 72.8 m), the heavier arrow with vanes would maintain its velocity better and win in the long run.

Considering nothing else, if you never shoot past 40 yards, feathers would be the way to go. Speed, however, is not the only consideration when choosing fletching material. Feathers are quite fragile and more difficult to attach to arrow shafts. They damage easily in rugged hunting conditions. In wet weather feathers go flat and lose their "steering" properties. Some weatherproofing products are available for feathers. But, in my experience, waterproof sprays are a temporary fix for a recurring problem. It's a nuisance to enclose feather fletching in plastic bags in most hunting scenarios.

Because feathers are so light, it's easier to achieve a higher FOC. Switching from vanes to feathers but leaving the shaft and broadhead the same, an arrow may increase FOC by several percentage points. The extra-nose-heavy flight and inherent arrow stabilizing characteristics of feathers will improve your groups.

The same textured surface of feathers that encourages arrows to stabilize quicker in flight and thus forgive shooting form errors, is also noisy. Feathers whistle somewhat in flight; perhaps alerting a target animal. Additionally feathers are noisy when brushed against a pant leg or bushes while stalking. Feather-fletched arrows are easier to tune because the feathers flatten when contacting any part of the arrow rest.

If you hunt in gentle terrain, arid conditions and never shoot past 40 yards, feathers would be an excellent choice to steer a hunting arrow.

Vanes

Vanes are considerably more durable than feathers. On countless occasions, I've thrashed arrows when fighting through alder thickets on wilderness hunts. Vanes are impervious to such a beating. Feathers in the same scenario would be torn to shreds and rendered useless. A quality plastic fletching is also impervious to weather. Wet or dry, hot or cold, there is very little difference in a

vane's ability to steer an arrow. Vanes are quieter in flight and don't rustle when bumped against branches or a pant leg.

Heavier vanes make achieving more FOC a little tougher. When a plastic vane makes contact with an arrow rest, wobbling arrow flight occurs; accuracy deteriorates rapidly. In other words, vanes don't stabilize the arrow quite as well or as quickly as feathers.

With sufficient fletching surface area, either material will stabilize and steer a broadhead-tipped arrow extremely well. You'd have to be capable of consistently shooting 2-inch (5-cm) groups at 40 yards (36.4 m) with broadheads to see much difference in the two materials' abilities to maintain accuracy.

I shoot feathers for indoor target and 3-D shooting. I believe they perform better than vanes at close range in ideal conditions when flight noise is moot. I hunt with vane-fletched arrows because they are maintenance free and out West I frequently make shots longer than 40 yards and in foul weather.

In a nutshell, regardless of shaft and fletching material, make sure your hunting arrows are extremely consistent in all aspects. The more uniform the arrow, the better chance of shooting tight groups. Tight groups lead to confidence and that helps you make the shot when it really counts.

Both vanes and feathers need ample fletching surface area to provide accurate steerage of a broadhead-tipped arrow.

CHAPTER FOUR

Broadheads: Practical Advice

I'd drawn a coveted permit for an archery-only Dall sheep area in the Chugach Mountains of south central Alaska. I went into the hunt convinced there were only three possible conclusions: The season would end, I'd die trying or a white ram would meet his maker! Fortunately, the only desirable conclusion occurred on the first day of the hunt.

Late in the evening I'd glassed up a lone ram with thick, dark horns that contrasted with his dingy white pelage. After a nerve-wracking, hanging-by-my-fingernails-and-boot-soles-while-pressing-my-face-against-the-cliff ordeal, I tiptoed up a staircase-like ledge close to the ram's last known position. The steep gully and cliffs were such that the ram would either be gone or right under my nose.

Without moving my head and only searching with my eyes, I was thrilled to see the ram feeding contentedly barely 20 yards (18 m) below me.

It was so steep, had I shot from where I stood, the arrow would have exploded into the volcanic rocks at my feet. When the ram shoved his head into an alder bush, I side-stepped to the cliff's edge, slowly drew my bow, picked a spot and released subcosciously.

The razor-sharp, broadhead-tipped arrow flicked through the ram's chest so swiftly he knew not his fate. The sheep merely lifted his head, curious of the dull "thunk" of the bow, trotted a few steps, walked a couple more and collapsed before a single drop of blood hit the ground.

That's what a well-placed, well-made broadhead can do–dispatch game swiftly and humanely.

The best broadhead for bowhunting is the one you are most confident with. With the plethora of choices available, what criteria does a bowhunter consider when choosing a broadhead? I believe there are eight crucial factors to consider: accuracy, sharpness, design/quality, flight noise, convenience, penetration, cut area and cost.

Accuracy

Broadhead accuracy–while hunting–is by far the most important criteria. If the broadhead-tipped arrow doesn't fly spot-on every time, nothing else matters. The only way to find out how accurate broadheads fly out of your hunting rig is to shoot several kinds and record group sizes. Not only must it fly like a laser-guided missile shot after shot and one broadhead to the next, it must do so under actual hunting conditions.

It's one thing to group broadhead-tipped arrows when shooting at a foam target while standing in the backyard during T-shirt weather. It's entirely different and considerably more difficult to get a broadhead-tipped arrow to hit tack-on while shooting at live game when sitting in a tree stand on a bone-numbing November morning. Broadhead forgiveness is crucial in my book.

Sam Miller, pulling broadhead-tipped arrows from a GlenDel 3-D foam deer target.

A lot of broadhead forgiveness is contingent on its aerodynamics and bow tune. Here's an example: When you're driving down the road on a hot summer day and playing "airplane" with your hand "flying" out the car's window, the "plane" flies true if you hold your hand and arm just right. This represents a broadhead-tipped arrow flying out of a well-tuned bow. When you slightly dip or lift your fingers, this makeshift projectile veers off course erratically. That's exactly what happens when shooting a broadhead-tipped arrow out of an untuned bow or with lousy shooting form: It causes erratic arrow flight. Also, more and larger blades will exacerbate this wild flight. Imagine playing "airplane" with a magazine-size piece of stiff cardboard. It would be nearly impossible to get that large-bladed projectile to fly in a stable manner.

I'm not saying you can't make a large-bladed head fly true. On the contrary, with good form and proper tuning, you can get most broadheads to fly well. However, arrow flight with a big, non-vented, wide-bladed broadhead is going to be harder to control compared to a narrower, vented-blade with a sleek profile. This is especially true when you are shooting at game when perfect shooting form is unlikely.

For shoot testing, I'd suggest borrowing used heads from a pro shop or friend. The other option, in spite of cost, is to buy at least three heads of several models you believe will work for your hunting needs. Shoot them and learn for yourself which head works best for you. This extra expense is a worthwhile trade-off in building confidence in your chosen equipment.

Sharpness

We frequently hear heads described as "scalpel sharp" and "hair-shaving sharp." Regardless of what you call it, every hunter should devise a personal method for checking sharpness and stick with it. For instance, lightly drag a broadhead blade across a newspaper's edge, or carefully drag it across a 45-degree-angled thumbnail, or safely shave some arm hair. If the blade bends paper, slips off the angled thumbnail or doesn't shave arm hair easily, it's too dull for hunting.

Closely examine several brands of broadheads before buying. Some manufacturers only grind their blades. Others grind, hone and strop their blades. These extra steps increase price, but they do help ensure precision sharpness. Be aware that just because a manufacturer's package says "razor-sharp blades," it does not make it so. I've found an alarming number of "manufacturer-ready" blades too dull for hunting. Take the time to check each and every blade for sharpness. If blades aren't sharp, discard or re-sharpen them.

I'm certain most of us have killed a deer or two with a less-than-optimally-sharp broadhead and gotten the job done. In spite of that success, there are several reasons for having acute blade-sharpness standards. Sharp edges reduce friction and increase penetration. Super-sharp blades are more likely to slice arteries and veins upon the slightest contact. Rubbery blood vessels roll or "give" without being sliced by dull blades. A finely honed blade makes a surgeon-like clean cut. This causes more profuse bleeding because there are no jagged edges for blood platelets to clot on.

Furthermore, clean and sharp cuts cause less initial trauma to the body's natural repair system. Thus, more profuse blood loss occurs quickly, before the animal's clotting mechanisms kick in to stem the blood flow. Conversely, if you happen to make a non-lethal hit, a super-sharp blade wound will bleed profusely at first but heal more quickly than a jagged one.

Treat every broadhead as if it is scalpel-sharp for safety's sake. However, it's your ethical duty to check every blade for sharpness. Also, realize improper storage and transit of blades can dramatically reduce sharpness—so can repeatedly pulling a broadhead-tipped arrow in and out of a dusty or wet quiver. Always keep your sharp broadhead blades in a rattle-free, dry container. Be meticulous about broadhead blade sharpness and the blades will take care of business on their end.

Design and Quality

Like bow and arrow selection, broadhead design and quality are personal choices. I've killed countless big-game animals with cone-tipped, pyramid-tipped, cutting-tipped and expanding broadheads. They all have one thing in common: With proper shot placement, they all harvest game quickly and humanely.

For confidence's sake, I want every broadhead to weigh within a grain or two of each other. During one examination of 125-grain (8.10-g) broadheads, I found some weighing as light as 120 grains (7.78 g) and others in the same box weighing as heavy as 131 grains (8.49 g). A 10-grain (0.65-g) variance can affect consistent accuracy—especially with a fast, light arrow. Perhaps more importantly, I believe the variance will erode confidence as much or more than it will accuracy at less than 30 yards (27 m). At longer ranges, that 10-grain (0.65-g) difference will show up in the form of larger groups.

Besides weight consistency, check for broadhead concentricity by spinning the broadhead-tipped arrow in top-like fashion. The smoother the spin and less visible the wobble, the more likely the broadhead will fly true shot after shot. If you get a wobble, try different broadheads with different arrow shafts. If one head continues to wobble after trying it on several arrows, the ferrule is probably bent. Sometimes you can look down the shaft/ broadhead to see which way the ferrule is warped. To straighten it out, carefully put pressure on the tip. Other times, arrow inserts are glued-in crooked and require more effort.

Always spin-test every arrow and broadhead combination. Don't settle for anything less than precise concentricity.

Broadhead toughness or durability is another factor worth considering. If, during your shooting tests, a particular style of broadhead falls apart after a couple shots into a foam target, what will

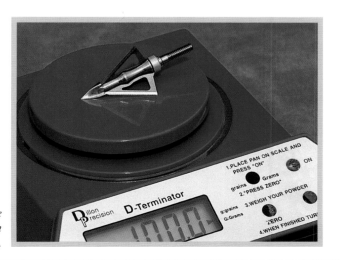

Here, a Rocky Mountain Ti-100 Barrie broadhead is weighed on a Dillon Precision electronic grain scale.

happen when shooting that head into the tough hide, dense muscle and thick bones of live game? I've had several broadhead blades chip, crack, bend and fall apart upon impact. These inferior designs never see the inside of my hunting quiver.

Also check the blade-to-ferrule fit. Some heads are manufactured to very tight tolerances. Others are so loose the blades almost fall out even when the broadhead is completely assembled. Spend an afternoon at a local pro shop and ask to assemble several brands of broadheads. Trial assembly also illustrates how convenient a particular head is to use. The difference in quality levels will soon become apparent.

Flight Noise

Do you think an owl could catch a mouse if the rodent could hear the owl as it swooped in? Probably not. And the same idea holds true in hunting.

The buzzing sound of a broadhead-tipped arrow in flight should not be ignored when selecting a broadhead—especially when hunting Pentium-processor-quick animals like whitetails and antelope. An excessively noisy broadhead may "telegraph" your shot just enough to cause a miss or, worse yet, a bad hit.

Find a safe backstop to stand behind and listen to different types of broadheads as they whiz downrange. Sound travels at 1,100 fps (335 mps), which is at least three or four times faster than your arrow. So bow and broadhead noise should not be taken lightly. Watching just one of your arrows darting toward a ducking whitetail should convince you to pay attention to flight noise.

Here, a G5 Montec 3-blade 100-grain broadhead is sharpened with G5's Diamond Sharpener.

Convenience

If a broadhead is difficult to assemble, dull out of the package or challenging to make concentric, forget it and move on. We are all too busy to fumble around with finicky broadheads. The last thing you want is a faulty broadhead eroding confidence while coming to full draw on your quarry.

Penetration

Yes, a cut-to-tip head penetrates better than a chisel point and a chisel-point head will likely penetrate better than an expanding head. However, with an average whitetail setup (60-pound/27-kg bow with a 400-grain/25.92-g arrow) the total penetration difference between one style of broadhead and the next is literally a fraction of an inch. My son, Tyler, killed his first deer at age 14 while shooting a rig that only produced 38 foot-pounds (5.26 kg-m) of kinetic energy. The chisel-point broadhead and arrow zipped through that mature whitetail doe like she wasn't there. When bowhunting large-bodied, heavy-boned game like elk, moose and brown bear, a cut-to-tip head may provide an extra few inches of penetration.

My motto is: Accurate shot placement reigns supreme. I believe improved shooting skills and being more selective with high-percentage shots can negate most penetration problems. However, we are all human and sometimes botch a shot. Therefore, choosing a broadhead that will perform flawlessly in worst-case scenarios is prudent.

To further illustrate how much more important shot placement is compared to raw penetrating power, look back in history. North American Indians killed deer with low-poundage bows using rock-tipped wooden arrows. The equipment we use today is far more efficient than their sticks and rocks.

Total Cut Area

This term refers to the combined area that all the broadhead blades collectively cut. I put this factor low on my list for the same reason I downplay the importance of penetration. With a well-placed shot, it doesn't really matter if vital tissue is cut with two or ten broadhead blades. Total cut area does become critical on marginal hits. Yet, only once have I experienced a significant difference in dispatch ability with less cutting surface.

Several years ago I shot a tough old mountain goat with a two-blade head. Ironically, the broadhead struck exactly vertically and directly in line with the animal's diaphragm. Thus, no lung or liver tissue was severed. Had I been shooting a three- or four-blade broadhead, a quicker recovery would have occurred. Had I made a more accurate shot, the number of broadhead blades would have been a moot point.

Some bowhunters are convinced a big, wide cut is better for a good blood trail and a quick recovery. However, if downrange accuracy decays by more than the extra fraction of an inch gained while using a larger diameter head, any gain is lost.

Expanding broadheads are a different matter. They generally fly well, yet cut a wide swath. While I have experienced less penetration when using expanding broadheads, this slight loss of penetration has not been detrimental. Early on, expanding or mechanical heads earned a bad reputation due to some poor designs and inferior manufacturing. Nowadays, there are numerous excellent mechanical heads. They are sturdy and easy to tune, fly well, group like field points and cut a good swath.

One caution: You may not get an exit wound when hunting with expanding broadheads (depending on the kinetic energy, shot placement, etc). This can be critical—especially when shooting at steep downward angles, such as from a tree stand or in the mountains. An animal shot with a high-on-the-body entrance wound and no exit channel can make recovery challenging.

If an expanding broadhead is legal in your area and your preference, I recommend using mechanical broadheads with the most kinetic energy you can accurately shoot.

Cost

It's ridiculous to pinch pennies on inferior broadheads when spending hundreds, if not thousands, of dollars on a quality hunt. For most of us, time is more valuable than money. So, if you are going to spend the time and money on a good hunt, don't squander it with cheap broadheads that are difficult to assemble or may fall apart upon impact with a game animal. Remember, though, high price alone does not guarantee superior quality. It's a good idea to evaluate every head, regardless of cost.

Summary

Over the years, I've had excellent results with Rocky Mountain, New Archery Products and Sonoran Bowhunting Products broadheads. However, it would be narrow-minded of me to think these are the only good heads available. I know many satisfied bowhunters using Muzzy, WASP, Rocket Aeroheads, G5, Eastman Outfitters, Steel Force, Magnus, Zwicky and other broadheads. Regardless of what brand you choose, make sure it meets your criteria so you have the utmost confidence.

Todd Wickens (far left) with his late-season mulie shot with an expanding broadhead. Lon (left) took this bull elk with a cut-to-tip broadhead.

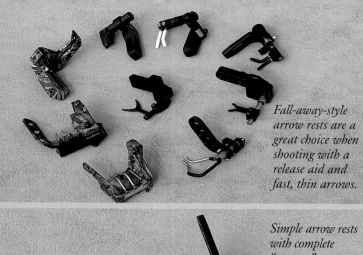

Fall-away-style arrow rests are a great choice when shooting with a release aid and fast, thin arrows.

Shoot-through-style rests are a good choice for those shooting aluminum arrows and a release.

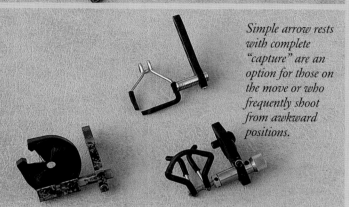

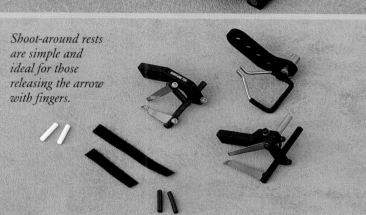

Simple arrow rests with complete "capture" are an option for those on the move or who frequently shoot from awkward positions.

Shoot-around rests are simple and ideal for those releasing the arrow with fingers.

CHAPTER FIVE

Accessories: Just the Necessities

On one trip while hunting Alaska's famous Kodiak Island for Sitka black-tailed deer, it rained incessantly for two days. A retriever can't get any wetter fetching a duck than I was during those forty-eight hours. Then, just at dark, the clouds vanished. A clear sky sent the temperature tumbling.

The next morning, with my breath smoking in the crisp air and the entire island dressed in frost, I stalked a beautiful Pope and Young–class buck. At 25 yards (23 m) and still undetected, I started to pull an arrow from the quiver. I tugged and tugged. The broadheads were frozen into the foam! When I yanked hard enough, an arrow came free but the cheap quiver bracket broke.

The deer was alerted to the noise but didn't spook. There I was, close to a buck with the quiver hood and arrows dangling from the quiver clip. I nocked an arrow, took aim and shot. In disbelief, I watched the arrow sail 3 feet (1 m) off target. The buck evaporated into the alders.

Dejected and frustrated, I sat down in the frosty tundra to figure out what had gone wrong.

Not only did the quiver bracket break, the cushion-plunger arrow rest froze solid, causing the wild shot. It only takes a couple lost opportunities due to faulty equipment to make you more critical of accessories. I'm certainly broad shouldered enough to take my licks when I'm at fault, but I won't tolerate shoddy equipment.

A good arrow rest, bow sight and peep sight dramatically improve a hunting bow's accuracy. A quiver and vibration-dampening devices make the bow a more effective hunting tool. Much beyond these five accessories and you start getting too complicated for serious bowhunting.

When choosing bow accessories, thoroughly inspect every product. How well constructed is it? How many screws and bolts does it have? Is it simple in design? Is it durable? Can you repair it while hunting? Most importantly, will the accessory function flawlessly in all hunting conditions?

Arrow Rest

The arrow rest ranks right up there with the arrow when it comes to crucial components for accuracy. There are so many styles of arrow rests now, it'll make your brain hurt like an ice-cream headache just sorting through them. When accuracy and hunting practicality become the litmus test, however, the decision gets easier.

An accurate-shooting arrow rest for hunting must have several key features:

• The rest must support the arrow during the initial stages of the launch cycle. For release shooters, vertical support is most important because there is very little horizontal paradox when the release jaws open. The string rushes forward and the arrow slides down the arrow rest support arms.

With a finger release, dumping the string causes the arrow to bend to the left (for a right-handed shooter). Thus, lateral and vertical arrow support is important.

• A good arrow rest must be designed with fletch clearance in mind. Vanes or feathers must either go between or around the arrow rest launching arms with minimal or no fletch contact. The less contact the fletching has with the rest, the more consistent arrow flight you'll achieve. That's why fall-away arrow rests are so popular. The launch arm drops away during the arrow's launch cycle before the fletching gets near. When set up properly a fall-away-style rest virtually eliminates fletch-to-rest interference. The instant I switched to a fall-away rest, my groups shrunk noticeably. And, I was already shooting very well.

• An accurate hunting arrow rest should be simple in design with few moving parts but still be very adjustable—horizontally and vertically. For example, the arrow rest I use has four parts, three bolts and one spring. I can tune a bow with this rest in minutes.

Another fall-away rest I examined has eleven parts, sixteen screws and one spring. Now which one of these rests is more likely to come out of adjustment?

• A practical hunting rest must provide excellent capture. That means the arrow will not fall off the rest during a stalk or if you have to draw the bow from an awkward position. Good capture also helps keep the arrow in place when it's windy. Most arrow rests use gravity and cradle arms to hold the arrow in place. This is fine if you always hold the bow upright and never encounter weird positions. Other arrow rests completely surround the arrow.

What I've found that works best (in conjunction with a fall-away rest) is to build a little "pinch bracket" just ahead of the launch arms. First, glue a 3/8-inch-wide (9.5-mm) piece of aluminum arrow (cut lengthwise so it forms a "U" shape) onto a felt pad. Next, attach this bracket to the riser shelf and cover the whole thing with adhesive-backed fleece. Finally, adjust the width of the pinch bracket to the diameter of the arrow.

When nocking an arrow, push the shaft down into the fleece-lined cradle. Done properly, you can turn the bow upside down without the arrow falling off the rest. When you draw the bow, the arrow rises with the launch arm of the fall-away rest. If you have to let down without shooting, the arrow drops right back into the cradle.

This pinch bracket coupled with a fall-away rest is the slickest, most accurate and practical hunting rest combination I've ever used.

Be forewarned: Fall-away rests do not work for finger shooters because there is no lateral arrow support when the arrow bends upon release.

Bow Sight

All my years bowhunting in Alaska taught me one thing: If a product failed, it could ruin an expensive hunt. This has solidified my preference for simple, solid and easy-to-adjust products. I know some folks think more bells and whistles make it better but my bowhunting time is precious. I'm certain yours is too. So why bog down your bow with a complicated sight or any other accessory for that matter? Sure as gravity, the one morning a dandy buck saunters by your stand will be the same day that whiz-bang sight goes on the fritz. My advice? Keep it simple.

Two good sight features that improve accuracy are a round pin guard and a bubble level. The round pin guard, when centered at all distances with a peep sight, acts as an additional anchor or aiming reference. A bubble level helps you hold the bow plumb and reduces left and right misses and really helps on sidehill and steep shots.

Pins

Select a sight with gang adjustment for windage and elevation. Make sure the sight also has easy, yet solid, individual pin adjustment, allowing precise pin placement. A good sight for hunting has a solid pin guard to protect the pins from brush and rocks.

How many pins will work best for your hunting style? If you mostly hunt from a tree stand in dense cover, a three-sight-pin model would suffice. Setting them for 10, 20 and 30 yards (9, 18 and 27 m) might work well. On the other hand, if you shoot a relatively fast bow with little trajectory between 10 and 20 yards, setting the sights for 20, 30 and 40 yards might be more logical. I hunt open ground out West. My five pins are set for 20, 30, 40, 50 and 60 yards (18, 27, 36, 45.5 and 55 m).

Regardless of how many pins and what distance they are set for, be consistent. Also, be sure to use the same-colored pin for each distance. I always know my top/green pin is set for 20 yards (18 m). At crunch time, I don't want to be confused by which pin is set for what distance.

Another consideration is pin diameter. Some people are very steady at full draw and want a small pin for precise aiming. Others feel a larger pin diameter covering more of the aiming spot disguises sight picture movement and thus gives them confidence in hitting the mark. Remember, the farther away your target animal is, the larger the sight pin will appear. Depending on pin diameter, all your pins

might cover the vitals of a buck at 15 yards (13.5 m), whereas the same buck's chest would be mostly covered at 60 yards (55 m) with just one pin.

Fiber Optics

With fiber-optic sights, the longer the fiber, the more light-gathering ability and thus a brighter pin glow. This can be advantageous in low-light situations. Pay attention to how well fiber optics are protected. By nature these fibers are fragile. A long fiber that's broken will only gather light from the break to the aiming tip. A good hunting sight will have sufficient protection for the fiber optics and if they do break, it should be simple to install a new one.

Peeps

Shooting a compound bow without a peep sight is like shooting a rifle with only a front sight. It'll work but accuracy suffers. When I bowhunted without a peep sight on the string, I just lined up the out-of-focus string with the pins and shot. As long as my anchor was consistent and I always aligned my eye on the same side of the string, I shot okay. Using a peep, however, I shoot much tighter groups.

Installing a string peep is a little thing that dramatically improves accuracy. It forces you to anchor the same way every time. If you don't, you can't see through the peep. This really comes in handy when shooting from odd angles and awkward body positions, which happens on just about every shot you're going to get at big game.

For hunting, a peep aperture of about 1/8 to 3/16 inch (3.2 to 4.8 mm) is a good place to start. The smaller the aperture, the harder it will be to see in low light but the more precise the aiming. A larger aperture will aid in seeing the front sight and target animal in low light but aiming is less precise and the target will appear out of focus.

The two drawbacks to using a peep are alignment and moisture problems. Once, while drawing down on a big old black bear, my string peep didn't rotate properly. At full draw I couldn't see the bear! I had to let down, twist the string

When choosing a bowhunting sight, remember that it should be sturdy, simple to adjust and provide a bright, clear sight picture.

Shooting a compound bow without a string peep can be done but not with the precision a rear sight provides.

and draw again. It was a frantic experience because the bear was about to catch my wind. Luckily, the peep straightened, and I cut the shot just as the bear smelled me. My arrow got there just in time.

There are a couple tricks to achieving consistent peep alignment. One is to attach rubber tubing between the peep and the top bow limb or bus cable. At full draw, the stretched tubing automatically aligns the peep. Another is to install a string made of two bundles of different material. One is wrapped clockwise, the other counterclockwise. Putting the peep between the two colors of string material usually balances the peep for good rotation. Another way to ensure good peep alignment is to shoot with a D-loop installed on the same plane as the peep. Attach a release to the D-loop and the peep will line up at full draw.

The first year I hunted with a peep sight, it cost me a tremendous buck.

It was a dank, drizzly day while hunting blacktails. The rut was in full swing. I came upon what may be the largest Sitka I've ever seen. I stalked him for hours. Finally, I got ahead of the buck, nocked an arrow and waited. Minutes later he wandered past me at 25 yards (23 m). He unknowingly stopped broadside and looked away. When I drew and tried to aim, I saw nothing but a blur! By the time I realized rain had clogged the peep, let down and shook the rain out, the buck had walked off.

Since then, I check my peep for rain or snow with vigilance. If for some reason this ever happens again, instead of letting down and shaking the rain out, I'll maintain full draw, bring the peep to my mouth and suck the moisture in. (This is quieter than blowing the rain out.)

Misalignment and moisture obscuring the peep sight picture can be eliminated with diligence. I believe the benefits outweigh the challenges.

Quiver

Basically, there are three types of quivers: backpack style, hip-style and bow-mounted.

Backpack Style

There are several designs of back quivers that frequently combine other backpack-like storage capabilities. These are convenient for carrying arrows safely, but they are a little slow and cumbersome in accessing an arrow. If you only hunt from a tree stand and never have to nock an arrow in a hurry, this style of quiver would be ideal.

Hip-Style

By using a hip quiver, you can slightly improve shooting accuracy compared to a bow-mounted quiver. The hip quiver keeps the physical weight of the bow to a minimum. Although a bow without a mounted quiver is less affected by wind, I suspect most bowhunters don't shoot well enough or far enough to really see much improved accuracy by keeping the quiver off the bow.

On the flip side, I find hip quivers cumbersome and noisy while moving. The arrows catch on brush and fletches wag when crawling during a stalk. Once again, if you only hunt from a tree, a hip quiver is an excellent choice. If you spot and stalk, backpack hunt as well as tree stand hunt, I feel a bow-mounted quiver is most practical. Besides, there are many quick-detach models of bow-mounted quivers that make it easy to remove the quiver once on stand.

Bow-Mounted

Bow-mounted quivers provide the most compact, convenient and easy access to arrows of the three arrow storage devices. Remember, if you initially set up, tune and sight-in a bow without a mounted

To keep a quiver hood quiet, wrap it with adhesive-backed fleece and line it with a vibration-dampening insert like this Sims NavCom quiver insert.

quiver and then attach a quiver full of arrows, your bow tune and arrow point of impact may be altered slightly—perhaps a couple inches at 40 yards (36 m). I shoot tournaments without a bow-mounted quiver, but it's a simple and prudent process to tune and sight-in your bow with the quiver attached. A month or so before hunting season, it's wise (and bolsters confidence) to set up and shoot your bow exactly the way you intend to hunt with it.

One way or another, you must carry at least a few arrows while bowhunting. For serious bowhunting, any type of quiver must do all of the following:

• Safely enclose broadheads.

• Remain quiet during the shot cycle and while you remove an arrow.

• Hold the arrow shaft and broadhead snugly but not so tightly you have to use game-spooking motion to free the arrow.

• Have as much distance between the broadhead hood and the arrow clip as possible for your arrow length (if it's a bow-mounted quiver). Those stubby bow-mounted quivers leave a lot of arrow dangling below the arrow clip. This causes the arrows to violently vibrate (which makes noise) during the shot cycle.

• Be practical to carry for your type of hunting.

Vibration-Dampening Device

These accessories reduce vibration and noise. It's astonishing to watch slow-motion video of a bow and arrow during the shot cycle. You don't otherwise realize all those sturdy metal and high-tech carbonate components vibrate like a guitar string. Vibration causes sound and that sound travels pretty fast—1,100 fps (335 mps)—so a quiet-shooting bow is paramount to not spooking the animal before the arrow arrives.

On one late-season mule deer hunt, a quiet-shooting bow saved my bacon. It was bitter cold and the mulies were rutting up a storm. About 1 p.m. on the first day, a wide-racked buck followed a doe right under my stand. His huge antlers, and the stop-and-go nature of chasing a doe, fueled my buck fever. I must have drawn and let down six times before he finally stood still long enough for me to shoot. I proceeded to miss him at 25 yards (23 m)—and 30 yards (27 m)! Normally I can hit a tennis ball at those distances.

The dull "thunk" from my simply set up bow never made either deer flinch. They just kept rutting. Finally, on my third attempt, I settled down and cut a good shot. I dotted the buck at 37 yards (34 m). With a loud metallic crack from a noisy bow I'm certain those deer would have spooked on the first shot.

A sound-adsorbing stabilizer is a good investment. It'll add to the overall weight of the bow but it will lessen noise at the end of the shot cycle. Also, a stabilizer helps reduce hand shock. This makes a bow more comfortable to shoot. Sims Vibration Laboratory's (SVL) rubber Limbsaver "mushrooms" truly dampen shot vibration. Besides putting them on the limbs, I put Limbsavers on my quiver and sight.

If you want to go the extra mile, put a layer of SVL's insulator wrap between every accessory and where it's bolted to the bow. Metal-to-rubber-to-metal doesn't vibrate as much as metal-to-metal. Once you have all accessories securely installed, hold the bow at the grip with one hand and, with the other fist, pound on the bow where the riser and each limb connects. Any excess vibration can be heard. Have someone help you by holding one accessory at a time (while pounding on the riser). The process of elimination will indicate the noisy culprit, and you can remedy the problem.

Installing Sims Limbsaver Ultras to each limb of a bow and attaching string silencers to the bowstring reduces the chances of a deer "jumping the string."

CHAPTER SIX

Traditional Archery

The generation you grew up in frequently influences your "path" to traditional archery equipment. Some of us grew up before compound bows and, thus, started with traditional archery tackle. Younger bowhunters may have started their archery experiences in the compound bow era and then "graduated" to a recurve or longbow.

I grew up in the days of solid-fiberglass recurves. My father and oldest brother belonged to a group called Indian Guides. It was a Boy Scout–like organization that respected and emulated Native American culture and equipment. They studied and then made their own fletches, arrows, bowstring and so on. I watched with total fascination. Just six years old at the time, I had a fire in my belly for archery.

Needless to say, I was disappointed when the club disbanded. Fortunately, my interest in archery and parental trust to shoot unsupervised and with buddies solidified my burning passion for the stick and string. In the family garage were hay bales backed with a 3/4-inch (19 mm) sheet of plywood and a rusty nail pinning an old cigar box to the hay. It was all I needed! I'd shoot until my blistered fingers turned to calluses.

When I'd break or ruin arrows, I'd spend lawn-mowing money to buy more 49-cent wooden arrows at a nearby hardware store. My 22-pound (10-kg), cherry red, Shakespeare fiberglass recurve is where archery began for me.

Equipment

Regardless of your beginnings, it seems most bowhunters are intrigued with the simple beauty of traditional archery equipment. If you haven't dabbled with a stick bow at all or traditional archery is your roots but you've been away from it for a long time, here is some basic information to get you started in the right direction.

Bow

There are many companies that make "commercial" or "factory" stick bows and countless others who "custom" create longbows and recurves. Most stick bows come in three common lengths: 58-inch (147-cm), 60-inch (152-cm) and 62-inch (157-cm). Much like compound bows, longer traditional bows have a less severe string angle when at full draw and, thus, there is less finger pinch. Longer bows are generally a bit more forgiving of shooter errors, too.

As a rule of thumb, choose the longest bow (limb tip to limb tip) that will still provide optimal bow limb flex at your given draw length. For example, if you draw 27 inches (68.6 cm) or 28 inches (71 cm), a longbow or recurve of 58 inches (147 cm) would suit you well. However, if you are long in the arms and draw around 30 inches (76 cm), a stick bow of 62 inches (157 cm) would be more ideal. As with most aspects of archery, there's a balance between bow length, draw length and draw weight that'll provide the highest performance from the bow, yet still be comfortable and forgiving to shoot.

Without question, the biggest mistake most newcomers make is to select a bow with too much draw weight. It seems to be a macho thing to shoot a heavy-draw-weight bow. But, remember, the accuracy that frequently comes with a more forgiving and lighter-draw-weight bow is so much more important than raw power. As I've mentioned elsewhere, a fast miss in not nearly as impressive as a slower, more accurate hit!

According to Fred Eichler, a nationally respected hunting outfitter and recurve shooter, who is well on his way to killing the Super Slam of North America's big-game species, "You can kill anything on this continent with a stick bow that draws between 45 and 60 pounds [20 and 27 kg]." Fred is

Longbow shooter Travis Fryman at full draw. Turkey bowhunter Mark Land (inset) admires his Merriam's gobbler shot with a Black Widow recurve.

6 feet 2 inches (188 cm) and 210 pounds (94.5 kg) but only shoots a 54-pound (24.3-kg) recurve. Eichler explained, "When a buck pauses with its vitals obscured, a stick bow of less draw weight is easier to hold back that extra second or two until the deer steps clear. Also, you must realize for most traditional bows being drawn in the 27-inch [68.6-cm] to 30-inch [76-cm] range, there is about a 3-pound [1.35-kg] increase in draw weight for every inch [2.5 cm] of increased draw length. That means if you don't draw to the same anchor every time, you are changing the dynamic arrow spine and arrow speed. It's much easier to be consistent with less draw weight."

When it comes to choosing a traditional-style bow, there are a few common traits to look for, beyond the sleek beauty of finely crafted wood. Most importantly, look for one that doesn't "stack." That means the bow should increase draw weight in a smooth and consistent manner up to your draw length and not have a sudden, disproportionate increase in draw weight during those last few inches before reaching full draw. It's kind of like test-driving cars. You may have to try several models before finding one that feels just right.

You should also choose a bow with minimal recoil or bow jump. Make sure the riser handle feels good in your hand. Eichler told me about a gentleman who

broke a bone in his wrist from shooting a 70-pound (31.5-kg) longbow! "The hand shock in that bow was so severe, it snapped a bone in the guy's wrist," Eichler said. "Now that's what I call mismatched shooter and bow. The best advice I can provide is to make sure you shoot a lot of different bows until you get a sense of what feels good to you."

Regarding bow material, there are traditional bows made from all sorts of woods—bamboo, Osage, maple, yew, etc. There are countless wood lamination combinations and even some made with layers of synthetic material. Eichler said, "I'm not aware of any specific combination of bow materials that grossly outperforms any other. It's more in limb and overall bow design where you get performance. Also, with the advances in technology, modern lamination adhesives and wood sealants make most all traditional bows impervious to weather and greatly reduce the odds of limbs delaminating."

String

There are two main types of bowstrings for traditional archery: the Flemish twist string and the continuous-loop style. The Flemish twist string is the most common and has been used on bows for about 200 years. Nowadays, these hand-woven or hand-braided strings are mostly constructed from B-50 Dacron or Fast Flight.

The Flemish string is the quieter of the two during the shot cycle. Also, the Flemish string is specifically woven so it can be twisted up, thus providing more flexibility when adjusting the brace height or fistmele. Most custom bows come with a Flemish string. A Flemish string does creep or permanently elongate more than the other option. However, if you leave the bow strung for several days and shoot it about 200 shots, the string will be pretty much "shot-in." You can milk a few more feet (meters) per second out of a modern recurve while using a Fast Flight string as compared to a Dacron string.

The other type of bowstring found on some stick bows is the continuous-loop or endless string. This is the same design used on compound bowstrings. Generally, many factory bows come with a continuous-loop string. This string is also a bit noisier and not really designed to be twisted extensively.

David Etherington safely strings a traditional bow using a bowstringer.

Since all traditional bows are shot with a finger release that may cause excess string wear, special consideration must be given to the string's center serving material. Many traditional shooters prefer the tough, abrasion-resistant braided-nylon material for center serving as compared to monofilament serving.

As a backup, make sure you set up and use a second string. That way if anything should happen to your primary bowstring while hunting, you have an extra that will perform in a similar fashion with minimal fuss.

If you happen to own or purchase an old recurve or longbow, remember that the limb-tip material on most traditional bows more than fifteen or twenty years old may not be made strong enough to handle a Fast Flight string. This string material doesn't "give" as much as Dacron. A Fast Flight string on an antique bow can actually cut through the string grooves at the limb tips and ruin the bow and/or cause personal injury!

Arrow

When thinking about traditional archery, a beautifully crafted, Port Orford cedar shaft with custom cresting comes to mind. Yes, wood arrows are pretty and have been effective hunting projectiles for centuries. There's a certain sense of pride when crafting your own wood arrows and some folks go so far as collecting fallen feathers from wild turkeys.

With that said, there is no way even the most precisely matched wood arrows can compete with aluminum or carbon shafts for consistent weight and spine. Also, a tough arrow is important to the traditional archer, especially those who do a lot of stump shooting. You need a durable shaft to take the beating. Aluminum arrows do bend, groove, dent and break but are super consistent in spine and weight. Also, the variety of spines available in aluminum shafts provides extensive latitude in finding a shaft with the perfect spine for your setup. Aluminum arrows shoot extremely well out of stick bows.

On the other hand, many traditional archers are switching to carbon shafts. So-called purists may turn their noses up at such a thought. However, carbon arrows are considerably more durable. And the stiffer material and thinner shafts provide better

penetration. Eichler is now shooting Easton's Slim Tech Axis carbon shafts from his recurve. "I've had excellent results in tuning and shooting carbon arrows with traditional bows. Most of all, I've noticed increased penetration with the smaller diameter shafts. This is an important factor, considering the fact that stick bows just don't produce that much kinetic energy. With the thin carbon shafts, I'm confident about shooting through any North American big-game species."

Another type of carbon arrow the traditional shooter should seriously consider is the tapered Grizzly Stik from Alaska Bowhunting Supply. These arrows are thick at the front and narrow at the back. They are heavy and straight; they tune easily, fly great and penetrate deeply into the toughest game animals. I have several stick-bow-shooting friends who swear by these relatively new shafts.

Of course, arrow weight plays a vital role in penetration as well. While most compound bow shooters hunt with arrows weighing between 5 and 8 grains (0.32 and 0.52 g) per pound (0.45 kg) of draw weight, stick bow shooters generally use arrows that weigh at least 8 to 10 grains (0.52 to 0.65 g) per pound (0.45 kg) of draw weight. All else being equal, a heavier arrow does penetrate deeper and absorbs more of the bow's energy, reducing hand shock and bow noise.

Pretty to look at but less effective than modern tackle is a knapped head of Onandaga chert (top); shaft of Viburnum wood, turkey feather fletching and a self nock (bottom).

Most traditionalists set up their arrows so they shoot with at least 10 percent FOC (front-of-center). Mark Land from Muzzy Broadhead company uses special brass inserts that weigh 100 grains (6.48 g). When he attaches a 125-grain (8.10-g) broadhead, his arrows are really front heavy but his Black Widow recurve is impressively accurate.

Because the arrow launched from a stick bow usually is shot right off the riser shelf, using feather fletches is imperative. The feathers flatten out when arrow-to-shelf contact occurs. This provides a much smoother launch. Good arrow flight would be extremely difficult when shooting a stick bow with vane-fletched arrows. Eichler prefers using 5-inch (12.7-cm) feathers when shooting aluminum or wood arrows yet opts for the 4-inch (10-cm) feathers for carbon arrows.

Interestingly, I just tested 4- and 5-inch feathers for flight noise at Sims Vibration Laboratory. With their sophisticated equipment I learned an arrow fletched with 5-inch feathers produces nearly twice as much flight noise as the same arrow with 4-inch feathers! In my mind, this noisier 5-inch feather-fletched arrow had better significantly improve arrow grouping to warrant the extra flight noise.

To dispel an old archery myth, slow-motion videography has proven it isn't necessary to shoot right-wing feathers and right-hand helical for a right-hand shooter or vice versa for lefties. Video shows the arrow doesn't start spinning until it is well past the riser. What's much more important is for the fletching to be consistent from one arrow to the next.

Broadhead

Most traditional shooters prefer two-blade, cut-to-tip broadheads because they provide a little better penetration than chisel-point heads. As stated in Chapter 4, the difference between a cut-to-tip and chisel-point head, all else being equal, is only a few percentage points. Yet when shooting a stick bow that doesn't produce a lot of kinetic energy, that extra penetration from the cutting-edge broadhead, albeit slight, may prove crucial.

In my opinion, expanding broadheads and traditional bows don't mix well. This combination is a disaster waiting to happen. Regardless of what

brand or style broadhead you choose, make sure it's hair-shaving sharp and flies with repeatable results.

Accessories

One reason many archers switch from the much more complicated compound bow and accessories to the traditional bow is its simplicity. Basically there's the bow, arrow, tab or glove, armguard and quiver.

• Choose a tab or glove that protects your fingers but not at the cost of losing sensation. Being able to feel the string is crucial to a good finger release. Although many traditionalists use a glove, during my thirty years of finger shooting, I preferred a tab. It allows use of bare fingers for other chores requiring subtle dexterity without removing the tab. Not so with a glove. Furthermore, the shooting glove frequently develops a groove from string pressure. This makes a smooth release more difficult. Regardless of whether you prefer a tab or glove, get a couple that fit well and provide the best-feeling release. Use them both so they are broken in. Then, keep one as a backup.

I learned the lost tab lesson the hard way.

On a Sitka blacktail hunt, I foolishly took off my tab instead of turning it around so it was out of the way while glassing up a dandy buck. Intent on stalking that deer, I walked away from the glassing perch. Returning to and finding that tab proved more difficult than killing the deer! I managed to shoot bare-fingered and made the shot. But, it really smarted

David Etherington pulls a Grizzly-stick arrow tipped with a Shokte broadhead from a Cat Quiver.

on the fingers. I wouldn't even have tried the shot except I stalked to within 12 yards 10.8 m) of the buck. Shooting with and without a tab changes finger-to-bowstring friction that may alter arrow flight.

• String-to-arm slap is much more common with stick bows than with compounds and, thus, most traditional shooters employ an armguard. Pick one that will flatten your sleeve and has a slick surface to reduce string friction yet doesn't constrict blood flow to the arm.

• As with compound bows, you have three quiver design choices: backpack style, hip style and bow-mounted.

If you have a one-piece stick bow, remember that any quiver mounted directly to the limbs will affect arrow speed and tune, and may alter the arrow's point of impact. There is a more dramatic difference in the combined bow-mounted quiver and arrow-weight ratio to the bow's physical weight with a stick bow than on a compound. You are generally shooting heavier arrows and a lighter bow with traditional gear.

Thus, make sure you practice with the bow set up as you intend to hunt. If you hunt with three arrows in the quiver and the fourth one on the bowstring, then practice with three arrows in the quiver. Go so far as removing the same arrow from the same spot in the quiver as you would on the first shot while hunting. This will ensure the bow's balance is the same whether you are hunting or practicing.

Eichler prefers using a Great Northern bow-mounted, quick-release quiver that attaches to the limb bolts of his three-piece, takedown recurve. "If I shot a one-piece bow, I'd think seriously about using a hip or back quiver," he said.

• Other accessories a stick-bow shooter may consider are things to make the bow shoot quieter and more comfortably. Placing adhesive-backed mole-skin along the last 4 or 5 inches (10 or 12.7 cm) on the inside of the limb tips to lessen string slap is a good idea. Furthermore, in my testing at Sims Vibration Laboratory, placing Sims String Leeches in the string and sticking their Ultra Limbsavers to each limb reduced both hand shock and bow noise by almost 300 percent when compared to the same bow without the dampening devices. I achieved similar results when shooting a longbow and recurve. Due to extreme hand shock and bow noise neither bow was very pleasant to shoot "straight out of the box." With the String Leeches and Ultra Limbsavers, both bows were a joy to shoot.

Shooting Form

According to Eichler, who has been successfully hunting and shooting a recurve for more than twenty years, "There is no wrong way or unacceptable shooting form for the traditionalist—as long as it's consistent. It doesn't matter if you hold the bow straight up and down, cant the bow, snap shoot or have a hard anchor. Just do it the same way every time and you'll be all right," he said. "However, holding the bow with a cant does improve the sight picture. You can see more of the target animal, whereas a more vertical bow would obscure your vision."

Regarding finger placement on the string, there is one crucial aspect that is frequently overlooked. Make sure the bow's draw weight is distributed somewhat evenly over all three fingers. If you don't pay attention, it's easy to load up most of the draw weight on the ring finger. This causes excess string oscillation during arrow launch, making bow tuning and accuracy more difficult. To check for uneven finger pressure against the string, draw the bow without an arrow nocked. Look into a mirror. Most likely you'll see the string bending more severely around your ring finger.

Due to the finger release and holding more weight at full draw when shooting a stick bow, a more violent arrow launch occurs. Thus, a smooth and consistent release is paramount to achieving any level of accuracy.

Make sure you are holding the draw weight with back tension and not arm tension. The finger release must be relaxed. Just drop the string and let the back muscles pull your hand straight back toward the shoulder. (For more information on releasing the arrow with fingers, see Chapter 8.)

Tuning

Much like a compound bow, tuning a stick bow is a unique combination of bow, arrow and archer that requires patience and diligence to find the optimum tune. Remember, any change to the setup may affect tune and ultimately the arrow's point of impact.

Many traditional archers "shoot tune" their bows, meaning they experiment with different arrow spines. They shoot and watch the arrow flight. Then go with the setup that provides the most accurate results. Eichler, however, prefers paper tuning much like compound shooters do. But there are some other considerations.

Brace Height

First, you should find the bow's "sweet spot." Each bow has a perfect brace height that makes the setup shoot its quietest and with the least amount of hand shock. Every stick bow has its own personality and the perfect brace height on one bow may not be the same for another, even if they have the same specifications.

Here are some tips to help you find the sweet spot:

• Shoot the bow with no string silencers and no vibration-dampening devices.

• Twist up the string, about three turns at a time.

• Shoot the bow to see how it feels and sounds. Those three twists will alter brace height by approximately 1/8 inch (3 mm).

• Keep experimenting with brace height up to 1/2 inch (12.7 mm) shorter and 1/2 inch longer than the manufacturer's recommended brace height.

At some point in that 1-inch (2.5-cm) variation in brace height, the bow will shoot considerably quieter and with noticeably less hand shock. Once you have found the sweet spot, you can set up the bow as you intend to hunt and continue with the tuning process.

Spine Variation

If you are going to paper tune, start about 6 feet (1.8 m) from the paper. This distance is far enough not to have archer's paradox affect tune but not so far that the feather fletching have taken over completely and stabilized the arrow. This gives you a decent read on how the arrow is launching out of the bow.

Vertical paper tears are corrected by moving the nock set. If the arrow is kicking tail-high, move the nock set lower and vice versa. Remember that if you shoot with the bow canted, poor vertical tears in paper are not solely caused by the nock set. For example (for the right-handed archer) an arrow kicking high-left, indicates the arrow is acting weak in spine, whereas a low-right paper tear indicates a stiff-acting arrow.

Most spine corrections and tuning improvements are achieved by shooting shafts with different static spine, changing the point weight and the arrow length. (See Chapter 16 for more details on how to alter the dynamic spine of the arrow.)

Riser Shelf Contact

Most factory production stick bows are made with a flat riser shelf. This causes a lot of arrow-to-shelf

contact that leads to difficult tuning. A nifty and simple trick to dramatically improve arrow flight is to glue a small length of 1/4-inch-diameter (6.4 mm) dowel (split in half) under the riser shelf padding. The arch of the dowel greatly minimizes arrow-to-shelf contact and will frequently solve most tuning problems.

Be sure to glue the flat side of the dowel against the riser shelf and place it in the center of the area on the shelf that receives the most arrow contact. The wear on the shelf padding and/or performing a "powder test" with your arrow will indicate the area of most contact.

Aiming

There are three widely accepted methods of "aiming" a traditional-style bow: instinctive shooting, gap shooting and gun barreling.

Regardless of which aiming method you choose, learn to "aim small to hit small." This means if you aim at an entire door, you'll be lucky just to hit the door. However, if you concentrate on hitting only the keyhole, you are much more apt to hit the doorknob! Select an aiming method that works for you and stick with it. Don't change your setup once you're tuned. And practice, practice, practice!

Instinctive Shooting

This type of aiming is achieved in a similar manner as throwing a baseball. Through much trial and error and extensive repetition you refine eye-hand coordination to the point where you simply look at the point you want the ball or, in this case, the arrow to go, and let 'er loose. It's as if the mind's computer visually recognizes when everything looks right and you shoot.

For instinctive shooters, distance is less important. You simply focus on the spot and release. For this reason, instinctive shooting may be the most versatile and effective aiming method when shooting at various distances. However, it takes considerable practice to achieve consistent results. Additionally, you can't expect repeatable results if you are constantly changing bows, arrows and accessories. Stick with one setup and learn to shoot it well.

For the best results with instinctive shooting, be sure to vary your distances and angles to the target frequently. Otherwise you will unintentionally program yourself to see only the correct sight picture for that one distance.

Gap Shooting

This aiming method refers to the visual gap seen between the tip of the arrow and the spot on the target where you want the arrow to hit. Gap shooting requires a consistent and solid anchor.

Initially you must discover what is called your "point-on" distance. Through practice, determine at what distance the arrow will impact the bull's-eye when aiming with the tip of the arrow point-on. Once you know your point-on distance, it's simply a matter of adjusting the gap, by raising or lowering the bow/arrow relation to the target, for varying known distances.

To be effective, gap shooters must memorize many different gaps and know the distance to the target via excellent range estimation skills or with a laser range finder.

Gun Barreling

The method of aiming a stick bow known as "gun barreling" refers to literally looking down the arrow as if you were looking down a shotgun barrel. With practice you learn to alter the arrow's height relation to the target to compensate for distance and trajectory.

The trick to making this technique work is employing a three-finger-under-the-arrow-style release and a very high anchor point (such as on the cheekbone). This visually puts the arrow directly under the shooter's dominant eye. Aiming right down the arrow can be very effective out to 20 to 25 yards (18 to 23 m). Beyond 25 yards or so, gun barreling becomes more difficult because the arrow obscures the target, due to the higher hold necessary for the dramatic arching flight path of the arrow.

Practice Regimen

Undoubtedly, shooting a traditional bow with consistent accuracy requires much more dedication and more practice than shooting a compound bow. While hunting and at tournaments, I've seen people shoot longbows and recurves with impressive results. But they didn't get them without considerable effort and honed skills.

Remember, perfect practice makes perfect. So, a few well-concentrated arrows will serve you better than gobs of haphazardly shot arrows. Twenty good arrows per day will suffice. If your life schedule doesn't allow for sufficient practice time, you should think long and hard about ever hunting with a stick bow. Even with tremendous practice, some folks just never become very consistent with a longbow or recurve. Thus, it's imperative to learn just how far you can always keep an arrow in the kill zone of an animal. Shoot only within your effective range and not one yard (1 m) farther.

Bill Morehead demonstrates good shooting form using a cheekbone anchor point.

Harry Williamson showing good shooting form.

CHAPTER SEVEN

Practicing Good Shooting Form

Most bowhunters don't know what good shooting form looks like or, more importantly, feels like. Sadly, they just haven't learned. In my experience, the average bowhunter acquires a bow to extend hunting opportunities beyond the crowded rifle season. Then, the new archer contorts his or her body to fit whatever bow is available and instantly gets caught up in achieving results—hitting the bull's-eye. This sequence is dead wrong. The bow must first fit the archer. And then, with good, repeatable form, accuracy will follow. Don't be goal oriented; be technique oriented! To make the shot count while hunting, certain repeatable shooting form traits must be employed. (It may be helpful to review Chapter 1 regarding proper draw length.)

Remember, if you are an experienced archer changing shooting styles, you should only alter one aspect of your form at a time. Take it step by step and start at least six months before hunting season. If you are a new archer, starting off correctly will be much easier than breaking bad shooting form habits later.

Dominant Eye

Before establishing good shooting form, the archer must first determine his or her dominant eye—the eye that controls the "eye" segment of hand-eye coordination. Most right-handed people have a dominant right eye or what is sometimes referred to as the "master" eye. The same is true for most lefties. However, there are some folks with a shooting conundrum called "cross-dominance." These people are right-handed yet have a dominant left eye or vice versa. This makes aiming and shooting with consistency more challenging. An archer with cross-dominance must either shoot with the dominant eye closed to make use of the more coordinated side of the body or switch to shooting with the opposite "hand" to make use of the master eye.

Many bowhunters shoot a compound with one eye closed and do quite well, especially when employing a string peep sight and front sight. However, those shooting without sights, on a compound bow or stick bow, should shoot with both eyes open. Two eyes provide much better depth perception and establish quicker target acquisition. Some shooters find it easier to close their dominant eye while others get better results by training the muscles on the "off" side of their body.

To determine your dominant eye, point an index finger at the corner of a wall (where the ceiling and walls join) with both eyes open. Pretend you are aiming at that corner with the index finger. Now, without moving your finger, close one eye and then the other. When the "sight picture" remains constant, that's your dominant eye. If, when you close a particular eye and it appears to magically shift the pointed finger out of the corner laterally, that's not your dominant eye.

Once you have determined your dominant eye, you can establish which eye and which side of the body to hold and aim the bow. Then, you are ready to start working on shooting form.

Basic Shooting Form

A great learning tool is to use a video camera. Set it on a tripod or have someone tape you while shooting. Then compare your form to the information provided in this book. This combination will provide you with a solid foundation in basic shooting form.

The following eleven steps will guide you to good basic shooting form: take a good stance, nock an arrow, attach your release or fingers to the string, dangle the bow for proper hand placement, slowly raise the bow to shooting height, slowly pull the bow to full draw, anchor, create a sight picture, aim, release, follow through. Let's examine each phase individually.

Step 1: Take a Stance

Initially, your stance should be with feet spread about shoulder-width apart; more than that creates a stance that won't be repeatable while in a tree stand. Be sure to stand erect with a straight head and spine, keeping knees slightly bent. For right-handed shooters, place your right foot a few inches ahead of the left and turn your chest slightly toward the target. This open stance will give you more arm-to-string clearance.

This is just a starting point in practice. Rarely in a hunting scenario will you be fortunate enough to shoot with ideal practice form. Regardless, you must start here so you know what a good stance and form feel like. Then, with experience, you can duplicate this feel when shooting from awkward positions.

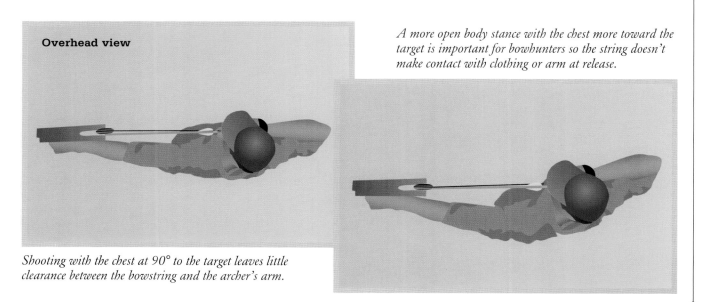

Overhead view

A more open body stance with the chest more toward the target is important for bowhunters so the string doesn't make contact with clothing or arm at release.

Shooting with the chest at 90° to the target leaves little clearance between the bowstring and the archer's arm.

Step 2: Nock Arrow

When nocking an arrow, most archers hold the bow horizontally with one hand, the arrow with the other. Then, they try to jam the nock onto the string with the broadhead flailing near their face. This method is unsafe, slow and clumsy–especially if you must hurriedly nock an arrow when cold, excited and in the presence of game. Additionally, since the bow is horizontal, the arrow quickly falls off most rests.

Here are four steps to a more hunter-savvy way of nocking the arrow:

A. Rest the bottom wheel of the bow against your upper thigh/hip to support the bow.

B. For right-handed shooters, hold the bow with your left hand and cant it to the right. This allows easy access to the arrow rest yet provides gravity's pull to hold the arrow on the rest.

C. Grab the arrow by the fletching with your right hand and slide the arrow shaft onto the arrow rest. If necessary, place the left index finger over the arrow to hold it on the rest.

D. Use your right hand and the arrow rest to guide the nock backward onto the string.

With practice this method of nocking an arrow is quicker and more accurate than stabbing the nock at the bowstring in a panic. It may give you a couple extra seconds to make the shot while hunting.

Step 3: Attach Release or Fingers

Practice placing your fingers or mechanical release aid onto the string quietly and, eventually, without looking. Some releases have an audible click or cocking sound. Figure out how to eliminate this noise or choose another release. Someday while hunting, you'll need to keep your eyes on the quarry and hook up by feel. Working on this no-look attachment technique in the backyard will make it automatic when hunting.

Step 4: Dangle Bow

After attaching to the string, dangle the bow on your fingers or release aid. Then, with even tension,

slowly pull the bow up against and into the yoke of your bow hand to achieve proper hand placement. Including this step in practice will help eliminate excess hand torque. It also helps train yourself to feel proper hand placement and thus dramatically reduce left or right arrow impact when hunting.

Step 5: Slowly Raise Bow

It's exasperating to put together a high-percentage shot opportunity at game only to telegraph your presence by thrusting the bow up to shooting height. If you consciously and slowly raise your bow to the intended shooting height and angle in practice, this stealthy act will occur naturally when hunting.

Step 6: Slowly Draw Bow

As with the previous step, you must learn to draw the bow in slow motion. Most game animals have excellent vision for picking up movement. Even near-sighted game like bears and pigs will spook at the quick movement of thrusting and gyrating a bow to full draw. This one aspect–holding and drawing a bow in the presence of nearby game–is what sets bowhunting apart from all other disciplines of hunting. If drawing the bow causes excess movement, you are shooting too much draw weight.

For the right-handed shooter, roll your right shoulder and back muscles up and then back to draw and hold at full draw. It drives me nuts to see people pull their bows to full draw using their bicep. Here's why: One, it takes more game-spooking movement to yank a bow back with arm and bicep muscles.

Two, it's impossible to draw a bow with the bicep and arm and then transfer the muscle tension to the shoulder and back–where the tension is supposed to be! Drawing with shoulder and back muscles can be achieved with substantially less movement. By maintaining back tension and keeping the arms relaxed, you'll achieve steady aiming and a surprise release. This is invariably the most accurate way to shoot a bow and arrow.

Step 7: Anchor

Anchor refers to a comfortable and repeatable location to place the hand of the drawing arm on the shooter's face, jaw or neck. I form a "J" with my right hand. The index finger is the stem of the "J," and the spot where my thumb joins my hand is the hook part of the letter. With palm facing down, I place this "J"-shaped hand under and alongside my jawbone for a consistent anchor.

When I shot with fingers, I employed basically the same anchor except the back of my hand was vertical and parallel to the bowstring. Some finger shooters put the index finger in the corner of the mouth, on the eyetooth or in the middle of the chin bone. Those using a strapless release frequently make a fist, turn it upside down and place the valley formed from the knuckles of the index and middle fingers against the jawbone. (For more information, see Chapter 8.)

Regardless of where and how you anchor, make it consistent. Without a repeatable anchor, your sight picture will alter, sending arrows to different points of impact at the same yardage. Without a solid anchor, you're not likely to hold the same

poundage at full draw. This will alter bow/arrow tune and cause erratic arrow flight and inconsistent points of impact as well.

Step 8: Create Sight Picture

Once at full draw, and anchor is achieved, create a repeatable sight picture. For me, this is centering the round pin guard of the front sight in the center of the string peep and then floating the correct pin on target. An instinctive or gap shooter may look down the shaft and then focus on the target the same way for each shot. A person shooting without a rear peep sight might look at the sights by consciously peering past the same side of the string on every shot.

Step 9: Aim

As with any other shooting sport, the process of aiming is the "eye" part of "hand-eye" coordination. The key to aiming a bow and arrow is not forcing the sight picture onto the target and then holding it there with brute force. It is not humanly possible to hold a bow at full draw perfectly still. However, with strength training, proper breathing and relaxing you can hold a bow pretty darn steady. Just let the sight pin gently float around your intended point of impact.

Fighting the bow to stay on target and then punching the release is a common mistake. I always bring my sight down through the intended point of impact and then slightly raise it back up to achieve the proper sight picture. Others prefer to come in from the side or bottom.

Regardless of how you aim, this one step of the shot cycle will be the only conscious thought at the moment of arrow launch. All the previous steps and the two remaining steps should occur on a subconscious level. If you are thinking about anything besides aiming when the shot goes off, you've had a breakdown in the aiming process and accuracy will suffer.

Step 10: Release

Whether with fingers or a mechanical release aid, the act of "loosing" the arrow toward its intended target is extremely crucial to accurate shooting. I

Here, 15-year-old Tyler Lauber demonstrates excellent archery shooting form. Notice the relaxed release hand.

won't go into detail about releasing the arrow here because Chapter 8 is dedicated to this key component of good shooting form. However, I can't emphasize enough how critical it is to establish a smooth, consistent release. Just like the anchor, an inconsistent release will be glaringly obvious downrange, with shotgun-pattern arrow groupings.

Step 11: Follow Through

If a gymnast doesn't follow through he or she will fall flat on the mat. If a golfer doesn't follow through, the ball doesn't carry well or travel in the proper direction. The same is true with archery, especially when hunting. Without proper follow-through, you'll feel like you've fallen on your face when shooting at game because the arrow did not fly to its intended mark.

As the arrow is launched and traveling down the arrow rest, follow-through begins. For consistent accuracy you must see and feel the shot to fruition. If your bow violently drops, jumps or kicks erratically off to one side your shooting form is poor and your follow-through improper.

Be sure to continue holding the bow at aiming height until the arrow impacts the target. The more distant the target, the more crucial this step becomes. Keep aiming until you hear the arrow impact the target. The only acceptable movement after the arrow is released should be the bow gently falling straight forward out of the bow hand (use a bow sling to keep from dropping the bow) and the release hand snapping directly back so the fingers or release touches your shoulder. If this doesn't occur, your follow-through is incomplete. Also, should your hand "fling" out to the side of your face instead of coming straight back, your follow-through is flawed.

In Summary

Whether you use this basic shooting form sequence or create your own, follow it exactly the same way every time you shoot an arrow in practice. Consciously think about each and every step while preparing the shot. When you get to the aiming step, aiming should be your only cognizant thought. All other aspects of shooting form should have been previously addressed so there's no need to distract yourself with those details. With proper practice, the release and follow-through will become subconscious acts and your arrow will find its mark with uncanny accuracy.

Advanced Shooting Form

Once you have good basic shooting form and have achieved some level of accuracy, you are likely to hit a "plateau." No matter what you do, you just can't shoot any better. When this occurs, you need to do something different. Here are some advanced aspects of shooting form you may want to consider when trying to improve your accuracy to an even higher level.

Research

To start your journey into advanced shooting form, study the photos in this book, go to your local archery shop and observe the posters of pro shooters or look online at professional archers at full draw. They may anchor differently and hold the bow with different finger positions but you'll see these key aspects of professional archery form: Most have their bow arm slightly bent, their bow shoulder and elbow will be rotated down and their torso and arms form a "T." Pros all have a relaxed grip on a thin bow handle. Also, they are so calm and relaxed at full draw it appears they could almost fall asleep!

Muscle Memory

It takes about 2,000 arrows shot with an identical thought process and consistent physical form to start gelling as a habit. You're unlikely to shoot that many times at game in your life. So, learning repeatable form must occur in practice. With diligent practice, you can train your body and mind to perform in a repeatable fashion. This is called muscle memory. When you do, the entire shot sequence, except aiming, will occur on a subconscious level. That way, while hunting, you don't have to think about anything except when to draw the bow, yardage estimation and picking a spot.

In short, it takes a lot of practice to train the mind and body to do things in a repeatable fashion. Moreover, when you start changing parts of your shooting form or routine, only change one thing at a time. Remember, it'll take considerable conscious effort to convert the new aspect so it becomes routine.

Body Position

With your eyes closed, come to full draw, settle into your best form and relax. Then open your eyes. The peep alignment and sight picture should line up perfectly. No body parts should have to shift or be forced to achieve an effective shooting position. Good form produces consistent accuracy while leaning out around a tree, kneeling or shooting uphill or downhill. If shooting in any odd position changes the arrow's point of impact, then your form is not consistent. The acid test of good shooting form is maintaining pinpoint accuracy while shooting from really weird positions, which is the norm when bowhunting.

To achieve repeatable form regardless of stance, form a "T" with your upper body. Your torso and spine represents the vertical part of the "T" while your arms form the horizontal line of the "T." We all have varying physical characteristics; just make the best "T" your body can. Make sure your bow shoulder is rotated down and relaxed. At full draw, the shoulder and elbow of the release hand should be slightly above but parallel to the arrow. If the elbow of your shooting arm is at about nose height, you're on the right track.

What happens from the waist down is not nearly as important as what happens from the waist up. Try to keep your torso at 90 degrees to, or slightly facing, the target animal regardless of whether that angle is up, down or canted to one side. Try to mimic level-ground torso shooting form by manipulating the lower body only. Keep the

upper body consistent. Bending at the waist and then leaning the torso to get that 90-degree angle most easily accomplishes this. Lots of practice is the only answer here because when it comes to a hunting shot, you don't want to draw the bow on the level and then bend at the waist to shoot out of a tree stand. In a hunting situation you must minimize movement by drawing in the awkward position yet still feeling the proper form to make an accurate shot.

Relaxation

It might seem odd but complete physical and mental relaxation while holding at full draw is one secret to pro-like accuracy. This starts with your head. It should be perfectly upright with neck muscles relaxed. Draw the bowstring to your face; don't move your face to the string. Don't cock your head or lean back. Look at Olympic skaters as an example: Their perfect balance starts with proper head position. If skaters spin with their head out of center, they fall over.

Two key components to relaxing at full draw are proper draw length and draw weight. If you are overextending to hold at full draw or holding too much draw weight, it'll be nearly impossible to relax. Too short of a draw length makes you feel bunched up and have to push and pull harder to maintain full draw. For me, I certainly notice the difference when shooting a bow that's 1/2 inch (12.7 mm) too short or one that's even 1/4 inch (6.4 mm) too long.

Remember, tense muscles cause shaking. Shaking causes an unstable sight picture. An unstable sight picture causes you to anticipate the release. Anticipating the release of the arrow causes anxiety about missing. With this sequence of events, the best you can hope for is intermittent success with "drive-by shooting."

Steady Hold

It's much more effective to find that perfect balance of draw length and draw weight. Then, relax, point the bow and let the bow shoot the shot. Too many times we force the bow to the aiming spot and then force the release at a fleetingly correct sight picture.

Here, Harry Williamson's excellent form illustrates the torso "T."

Besides strength training, so it's easier to hold at full draw, there are some tricks to holding steady. Once again, start with your eyes closed. Come to full draw and settle into your best form. Your muscles and bones are balancing and aligning naturally to be steady under the load. When you open your eyes, you'll be surprised at how steady you are.

The problem comes when you add aiming to the process. Most likely you weren't pointing where you wanted the arrow to hit when you opened your eyes, so you forced the bow on target with arm strength. Unfortunately, when you do this you are degrading your natural muscle and bone alignment, and steadiness turns to shakiness. So, the best approach is to maintain the steady shoulder/arm alignment but pivot at the waist and adjust aiming with your torso.

Aiming

Now that you've learned to hold steadier, the next step is aiming more effectively. Here's a little trick I learned from seven-time world archery champion, Randy Ulmer. He whole-heartedly agrees with the idea of aiming with your torso. In fact, he takes it one step further. Ulmer suggests you mentally split your body in half from head to toes. For a right-handed shooter that means mentally encourage the entire left half of your body to become inert. Then, aim with just the right side of the body, particularly the right shoulder. The first time I tried this, I was amazed with the results. I was shooting at 40 yards (36 m) and consistently grouped four arrows in the size of a golf ball!

Another key element to aiming is visual focus. Remember these six things:

• Focus on the target animal before the shot.

• Focus on the target animal while drawing the bow.

• Focus on the target animal as you align peep sight, pin guard and pin on the target animal.

• Focus on a single hair or a tiny spot on the target animal.

• Focus on the target animal as you release the string.

• Focus on the target animal and sight picture until the arrow impacts the target animal.

Get the hint? FOCUS!

All this focusing should occur in a rhythm, too. Most archery experts agree the shot sequence, from start to finish, should be a continuous, fluid entity. If you stop and start any part of the shot sequence it takes extraneous effort and you'll be less accurate. The longer you try to aim, the less accurate you'll become. It's best if your entire shot sequence—from drawing, anchoring, aiming, releasing and following through—takes between five and eight seconds. If your shot sequence takes longer than that, lactic acid builds up in the muscles and you become too shaky to hold steady. Also, if your shot sequence takes much longer than eight seconds, you probably don't trust that the movement you see in the sight picture will result in an accurate shot. If that's the case, move closer to the target, let the sight pin float on target and let the bow shoot the shot. Once you can do that, slowly increase the target distance.

Breathing

With most shooting sports that require precise aiming, developing a breathing pattern is crucial to success. My routine is to take three deep, slow breaths by inhaling through my nose and exhaling out my mouth. As I'm inhaling the third breath, I draw and anchor. Then I partially exhale and postpone breathing for the five to eight seconds it takes to execute the shot.

Sight Picture

The most consistently accurate way I've found to aim a compound bow is with a peep sight in the string and pin sight/bracket attached to the bow. I bowhunted for years without a peep sight and killed numerous big-game animals. My groups instantly shrank, however, when I did install a string peep. This rear sight forced me to maintain consistent form, especially in steep terrain. The peep acts as an additional anchor.

Normally, bowhunters center the pin in the peep aperture and then put the pin on target. This works pretty well. However, when you shoot at longer distances, 50-plus yards (45.5 m), you must "float" your anchor to get the lower pins to center in the peep. The slower your arrow and the more distant the target, the more pronounced this will become.

The easiest way to float your anchor is to slightly open your mouth while at full draw. This moves your jaw/anchor and allows you to shoot with the longer-distance pins in the center of the peep. If you don't anchor off your jaw, you may have to free-float your anchor hand to center the pin in the peep, and that will dramatically reduce accuracy.

PRACTICING GOOD SHOOTING FORM

One way to achieve a more consistent sight picture is to use a pin sight with a round pin guard. By experimenting with the peep aperture diameter and adjusting the pin sight bracket closer to or farther from the bow, you can create a sight picture where the round pin guard exactly fills the peep aperture while at full draw. Then, if you line up the pin guard circle with the peep circle, you've created another constant while aiming. With this method you do not center the chosen pin in the peep. You center the pin guard in the peep.

As with all changes to your shooting form or aiming process, it takes time and conscious effort to adjust. The benefits of this method are: One, you can use a larger peep that makes it easier to see in low light situations; the larger peep aligned with the round pin guard allows you to see all the pins all the time. This will reduce the chance of using the wrong pin when hunting. Two, you don't have to float your anchor to center the pin when shooting at longer yardages. Three, and most importantly, it's visually easier to verify the pin guard is centered in the peep. That translates into more accurate shooting.

The very best combination for a bowhunter is having a rear peep sight and front pin sights.

SHOOTING FORM ROUTINE

Be sure to develop a mental list of your shooting form procedure. For example, here's my shooting form process:

1. Stance—shoulders over hips, hips over feet.
2. Hook release to string.
3. Dangle the bow's weight onto the string.
4. Put tension on string to pull bow up into bow hand for consistent hand placement.
5. Slowly raise bow to target height.
6. Slowly draw bow—as if a buck is present—with back and shoulder muscles.
7. Anchor—release hand touching jawbone with light, consistent pressure; string lightly touching end of nose.
8. Double-check to ensure I'm not gripping the bow; the bow hand should be completely relaxed.
9. Center round pin guard in peep.
10. Relax left side of body as much as possible.
11. Adjust aim by rotating torso at the waist if needed.
12. Aim with right shoulder.
13. Get pin close to aiming point—let it float; don't force it to stay perfectly still.
14. Consciously start pulling with back tension.
15. Switch conscious mind to aiming, aim, aim, aim—release is a surprise.
16. Follow through until the fingers of the right hand touch shoulder.
17. Keep bow arm at shooting height until arrow impacts target and bow falls forward.

Whew! That's a lot to remember, and precisely why you want to have a routine to train your mind and body to perform the shot sequence the same way every time. Within a couple weeks—or however long it takes to shoot about 2,000 arrows with diligent concentration—your shooting form litany will start to become second nature.

It's sort of like when you first learned to drive a car. Early on, you had to think about mirrors, seat belts, steering, shifting, breaking, etc. Now, you just hop in the car and, before you know it, you're at your destination with very little conscious thought to the driving process.

That's the way you want your shooting form—so well practiced and consistent that when a deer presents a shot, you don't have to think about anything except picking a spot and aiming. The rest of the shot sequence should be automatic.

CHAPTER EIGHT

Releasing the Arrow

It's difficult to determine which aspects of shooting an arrow are most crucial for the bowhunter, but when and how to release the arrow in the presence of game is critical to accurate shooting and, ultimately, a humane harvest. There's a monumental difference between loosing an arrow at a three-dimensional foam replica of a deer and shooting at a living creature with warm, red blood coursing through its arteries. The target will stand there indefinitely and there's no need to hurry the shot. Wild game may or may not stand around long enough to release an effective arrow. It's your duty as an ethical hunter to determine when it's humane to release an arrow with the intent to kill a game animal. When to shoot is covered in Chapter 19, Moment of Truth. This chapter concentrates on how to release an arrow for consistent accuracy, whether you're a finger shooter or a release shooter.

Finger Shooting

I'd like to say I stay calm and concentrate well every time I shoot at game in nerve-rattling conditions and release the arrow on a subconscious level, but I'm not a very good liar. Regardless, loosing the arrow subconsciously while being totally focused on aiming is the best way to make the shot on a target or on game.

One of the best shots I ever made on game as a finger shooter occurred on a moose hunt in Northern Alaska with my good friend, Phil Lincoln.

I'd glassed up a monster bull cruising for cows along a thickly wooded river corridor. I tried catching up to the bull, crossing the thigh-deep river once and literally swimming that icy vein another time. With his long legs and fluid stride, I was no match to keep pace with the rut-driven bull. Completely drenched and dejected, I slogged back upstream toward camp and some dry clothes. Phil caught up with me and, while hiking, we heard the unmistakable sound of moose antlers crashing together! We waded across the river again and never stopped to dump water out of our boots. The stalk was elementary. As Phil said, "You could've walked in there with a marching band."

This was no sissy sparring match. It was a full-blown fight. There were 3,000 combined pounds (1,350 kg) of fighting protoplasm standing head to head. With bulging eyes on fire, they were pushing, shoving, grunting, blowing snot and splintering downed logs with flailing hooves as if it were kindling!

If their shear strength and the violent fight wasn't enough to intimidate a bowhunter, the 69-inch-wide (175 cm) antlers of world-record-class proportions on my bull should have been.

However, during a pause in the fight, I estimated the yardage at 30 yards (27 m), calmly drew my bow, anchored, picked a spot and released without even realizing it. The arrow buried fletch deep behind the bull's shoulder in the exact spot I was aiming. Later, Phil told me the arrow had hit exactly where he was looking, too. Perhaps our combined focus helped the arrow fly to its mark.

Finger Tab or Glove?

There's something unique about how an individual's fingers, short and fat or long and skinny, meld to a tab or glove and how they wrap around the bowstring. Luckily, there are numerous designs of finger tabs and gloves for the finger-shooting archer. I've tried several different gloves but never found one I liked. That doesn't mean, however, that a glove isn't right for you. Try a few different ones and go with what feels right.

During my thirty-one-year tenure as a finger shooter, I used all sorts of tabs. My all-time favorite was the Fab-Tab by Saunders Archery. It's made of a synthetic, waterproof material backed with a thin strip of leather and has a "can't pinch" device that keeps your index and middle fingers separated so as not to pinch the arrow's nock at full draw. The plastic surface is super slick and creates a consistent release, regardless of weather.

Keep wet-and-freezing or hot-and-sweaty conditions in mind when selecting a finger tab or glove for hunting. Will you be able to shoot with a tab over a regular glove in bitter weather? Will your fingers slip out of the individual ports of a shooting glove when drenched in sweat or rain?

Regardless of whether you prefer a tab or a glove, the universal features needed for bowhunting are:

• Thin enough so your fingers have a really good, sensitive feel of the string.

• Thick enough to protect fingers during the draw and release phases of the shot.

• The surface provides a consistently clean, smooth release.

• Fits comfortably so it becomes an integral part of the release hand.

A quality finger tab, like this Black Widow Tab, must perform consistently in all weather conditions.

Anchor Options

There are several tried-and-true methods of anchoring when employing a finger release for archery. I always put my middle and ring fingers underneath the arrow's nock and the index finger above. Then, at full draw, I put the curled tip of my index finger in the corner of my mouth. Additionally, I formed a "J" with my thumb and vertically aligned fingers and hand. I placed the curve of the "J" on my jawbone. This, combined with the index finger in the corner of the mouth, made for a solid anchor.

I won seven Alaska state archery champion titles with this finger-shooting anchor so it must be quite consistent. If I were to start over as a finger shooter, I would use the "two fingers under, one finger over" format, but I'd anchor by putting the curled tip of my index finger in the front or center of my chin and touch the string to the end of my nose. Many Olympic archers use this anchor so it must be solid and repeatable.

Some archers use all three fingers to draw the bow. Then, once at full draw, they straighten the index finger and only release the string with the two fingers below the nock. This is a viable option for those with a long draw length. Remember, the longer the draw, the more severe the angle of the bowstring. Thus, releasing with two fingers instead of three will reduce finger pinch. Also, many bowhunters place all three fingers under the arrow. Try all the variations illustrated in this chapter until you find one that is comfortable and easy to duplicate every shot.

Releasing

Most finger shooters place the joint or very near the first joint of the fingers on the string and then form a hook to pull back and hold the string. The key to a consistent and smooth finger release is having a relaxed hand and fingers, yet comfortably holding the draw weight of the bow. Make sure the back of your hand is very straight and not tense; otherwise, you'll put excess torque and twist on the string. That's why many beginning archers have trouble keeping the arrow on the rest. Their hand torque is twisting the string and pulling the arrow off the rest.

The best way to describe a good finger release is "dropping" the string. You literally relax the fingers in a slight downward motion. Then, the stored energy of the bow thrusts the string forward and past the relaxed fingers. The more relaxed your release hand and fingers and the less overall lateral movement involved in releasing the arrow, the more consistent you'll be.

 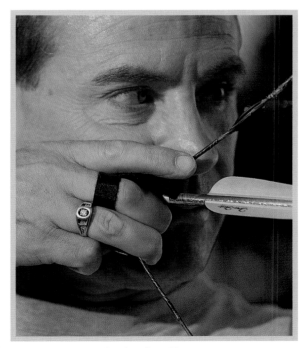

Josh Jones (left) illustrates the index-finger-to-chin, string-to-nose-style of anchor. Harry Williamson (right) demonstrates another style of anchor—he removes the index finger after drawing and then holds the draw weight and releases the arrow with just two fingers.

Regarding the mental aspect of releasing an arrow when finger shooting, it's best if you learn to release the string in a subconscious manner. Your conscious mind should be focused on the aiming process only. Releasing subconsciously when the sight picture is correct is the most consistent and fastest route to accurate finger shooting. Practice releasing the arrow with your eyes closed until you learn to feel a good release and don't have to think about it. Of course, a close, safe backstop is needed for practicing blind.

I've seen some horrible styles of finger release over the years but the least effective is to intentionally move the fingers out and away from the string. This causes the string to violently bend around the fingers, making the arrow launch quite wobbly.

It's physically impossible to release a bowstring with fingers and not have the string bend around the fingers and thus whip the arrow laterally to some extent. This is called archer's paradox. The string and arrow actually bend in the opposite direction to which the fingers are released. Obviously, the less lateral movement of the arrow during the launch, the cleaner the arrow flight you'll achieve.

Remember, any air drag on broadhead blades will cause the broadhead to compete with the fletching for steering command. When this happens, consistent accuracy suffers. Also, archer's paradox is the reason a finger shooter needs to use an arrow rest with lateral support and some type of cushion plunger to help absorb some of the sideways motion of the arrow during launch.

Follow-Through

After you have loosed the string with a relaxed, minimal dropping of the fingers, you must follow through. A good, consistent follow-through after the release is the string hand and fingers coming straight back until the fingers touch the shoulder. If your hand and fingers flap out to the side and away from your face, downrange accuracy will suffer considerably.

If you are holding the bow at full draw with back and shoulder muscles, as you are supposed to, when you drop the string, the release hand should snap straight back naturally. In short, follow-through isn't really a separate entity; it's the continuation and conclusion of the release.

Release Shooting

The best shot I ever made using a mechanical release aid took place in the Colorado high country on an early-season mule deer hunt with my good friend, South Cox. For the seven years I'd been using a mechanical release aid, prior to this shot, I'd struggled mightily at times with target panic and punching the release, both in practice and, even worse, when shooting at game. To say it was a challenge to switch from finger shooting to a release is an understatement!

Anyway, I'd dedicated hundreds of hours that spring and summer to learning to shoot with back tension that creates a surprise release. By the time hunting season rolled around, I was shooting the best I've ever shot.

It was about noon on the fourth day of that hot-weather hunt when I glassed up nine fuzzy-antlered bucks milling and feeding their way toward a pond for a midday drink. In sock-covered feet, I slipped down the ridge trying to intercept the deer before they reached the pond. After more than an hour of them nibbling, bedding down and then casually wandering toward water, I'd finally slithered into position for a shot.

Previously, I'd checked the distance with a laser range finder. The biggest buck was 47 yards (43 m) away. When the deer stood up from his temporary bed and looked downhill at the other deer, it was the moment I was waiting for.

I don't even remember drawing, anchoring or anything. All I remember was letting my 50-yard (45.5-m) pin float on his brisket just behind his shoulder and internally saying "Aim, aim, aim."

The next thing I saw was the arrow just as it impacted the deer. It was a perfect pocket shot and the first time I'd ever shot a big-game animal using back tension and a surprise release. It felt good!

Release Aid Types

The beauty of a well-made release aid is the consistent release and, thus, smooth launch of the arrow. Moreover, when the jaw of the release opens, the string thrusts straight forward with minimal archer's paradox, as when finger shooting. These aspects create very repeatable, clean arrow flight. That translates into improved downrange accuracy.

The improved accuracy of shooting with a release aid is the reason archery organizations have different shooting classes; so finger shooters don't have to compete against release shooters. There are a few top-notch finger shooters who might compete with release shooters on a given day but invariably those employing a mechanical release aid score higher in all forms of archery competition.

There are enough shapes, sizes and designs of release aids to make your head spin! There are three basic designs: handheld T-shaped, concho and wrist-strap.

• Handheld models are ergonomically designed to feel comfortable in a closed, yet relaxed, hand. They are triggered either by thumb or pinky finger. Some models allow you to switch triggering methods. The handheld designs are most popular with tournament archers. That should speak volumes about how accurate they are.

Although I do believe this is the most accurate style of release aid, it has drawbacks for hunting. If you're anything like me, constantly forgetting or misplacing things, a loose release aid seems like a disaster waiting to happen! I believe a handheld release aid

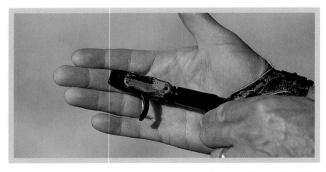

For proper fit (top), pull tightly against release head to simulate the bow's draw weight. Under tension, the release aid jaws should be between the middle and end joint of the middle finger. A handheld release (bottom) being attached to a D-loop.

must be kept in a lose-proof yet easily accessible and quiet pocket to be practical for bowhunting.

Also, in some hunting situations, just that extra time, movement and noise of reaching in a pocket for a release aid could foil the shot. I can't imagine continuously holding onto a cold chunk of metal while in a tree stand. Sure as gravity, I'd drop the darn thing just as a buck appeared!

Furthermore, when crawling on hands and knees during a stalk, it would be difficult to keep the release out of the dirt or snow. Once again, you'd have to keep it in a pocket and then fish it out and attach it to the string at the last moment. The only way I see a handheld release being practical for hunting would be using a design with a closed jaw that could be attached to a D-loop so the release aid dangled off the string at the ready instead of in a pocket. Or, there are some handheld release aids that are attached to a wrist strap with a cord.

Maybe I'm making it more complicated than necessary. But I'd think long and hard plus talk to those who use handheld release aids for hunting before I incorporated one of them into my bowhunting equipment.

• Concho-style release aids are actually handheld also. They have a post or stem that you grip with the palm of your hand. By design you must continue the tightly clinched hold. This flies in the face of relaxing at full draw and impedes accuracy. For this reason, concho-style release aids are a dying breed.

• Wrist-strap designs employ an index-finger trigger similar to that of a gun. They have one or two jaws that attach to the string or a D-loop and are the most popular and practical for bowhunting. They might be a tad less accurate in tournament shooting scenarios. But, in my opinion, their bowhunting advantages far outweigh the limitations. One advantage is, once attached, the wrist strap keeps the release ready and not likely lost.

I adamantly believe bowhunters concerned with accuracy and filling their tags should only use a wrist-strap-style release that fastens around the wrist with a buckle and not Velcro. The buckle is quick, quiet and, most importantly, it's easy to duplicate snugness on the wrist by using the same buckle hole each time you strap it on. Pick one with a stout leather or leather/synthetic composite. You don't want a buckle strap that'll stretch or you defeat the purpose—a repeatable snugness for a consistent anchor.

A mechanical release with a Velcro strap is more time consuming and difficult to put on. More importantly, adjusting the Velcro to the same tightness each time you shoot is difficult. When the wrist strap fits differently, even a little, you are effectively changing your draw length and shooting form. That results in an altered anchor and could change arrow tune and ultimately the arrow's point of impact.

Also, Velcro is noisy to strap on and during use. Many times during tournaments, I've heard other shooters' Velcro straps make noise as they came under tension while drawing. I feel this noise could telegraph your presence to alert quarry and increase the odds of it jumping the string.

Besides a quiet buckle strap, a hunting-smart release should have a quick, quiet manner to hook up to the string or D-loop. The jaw or jaws must be smoothly machined to minimize string wear. And, it should have an adjustable trigger with imperceptible trigger travel. Using a release that has considerable travel in the trigger before it goes off will cause you to anticipate the explosion of the shot. If you are anticipating when the release will go off, your conscious mind isn't focused on aiming. Less-than-desirable results will follow.

Look for a release that has plenty of length adjustment from the wrist strap to the head so it'll accommodate your hand size. I also like releases that have some sort of free-floating head that'll twist easily while drawing and anchoring. A release with a totally rigid head may bind against the string and cause unnecessary torque during the launch cycle.

Another consideration when choosing a release aid is the distance between the trigger and jaws. The more distance between the two, the shorter it will make your effective draw length. All else being equal, a 1-inch (2.5-cm) increase in draw length translates into an arrow leaving the bow between 7 and 12 fps (2 to 3.6 mps) faster (depending on bow design). That slightly flatter trajectory may help keep your arrow in the kill zone of an animal when guessing yardage while hunting. The trigger-to-jaw distance is particularly important to small-statured people like me where every bit of draw length is crucial.

My current release is a custom combination of a Tru-Fire Evolution buckle strap and a Carter Two Shot release head. The Evolution strap has a unique "arrowhead" tab that keeps the strap contained within the buckle at all times. I simply thread my hand through the strap "hoop," pull the

tab to the desired tightness, and buckle up! The Evolution consists of leather, padding and a layer of ballistic nylon that minimizes strap stretch while drawing and holding at full draw.

The Two Shot Carter release head is machined to perfection. The trigger is easily adjustable with imperceptible trigger travel. It provides a crisp release that melds nicely with my back-tension shooting style. I can attach the Two Shot to the string's D-loop silently. The built-in safety is well positioned and practical to use.

Release Aid Fit

No matter what brand of release aid you choose, how it fits in your hand is important to comfort and repeatable shooting form. With handheld releases, you're pretty much stuck with the fit and feel as they're made. Be sure to try several styles and pick the one that feels best and that you believe will improve accuracy.

With wrist-strap releases you want one with an easy, yet secure, method of adjustment. The strap should be snug but not constricting. Also, when pulling the release head tight against your flat, extended hand (imitating the tension of drawing the bow) the jaws of the release should line up

Josh Jones illustrates the hand-to-jaw, nose-on-string style of anchor with a caliper release aid. All the bow's tension is on the wrist, which creates a very repeatable shooting form.

somewhere between the first and second joint of the middle finger. By adjusting the strap-to-head length in this manner, you'll be at a good starting point for a comfortable reach to the trigger. It may take several adjustments to get a wrist-strap release to fit your face and hand for a repeatable anchor.

Anchor Options

Like finger shooting, there are several ways to anchor when shooting with a release. With a wrist-strap release, I form a "J" with my thumb and hand. The curve in the "J" where my thumb turns into my hand fits nicely against my jawbone for a comfortable and repeatable anchor. Some archers extend their thumb, making an "L" with the hand and then place the meat of the thumb on the back of the neck.

It's okay to clinch the release while drawing the bow. Once at full draw and anchored, make sure your entire hand is relaxed and the wrist supports the tension of the bow. A relaxed hand greatly reduces any torque the release may impart on the string and arrow.

With handheld release aids, you can usually find some combination of jawbone-to-knuckle-valley on the back of your hand that's comfortable and easy to repeat. Try it with your thumb knuckle pointing down, horizontally or at some angle. What works best for me is to put the knuckle valley between my index finger and middle finger against the back of my jawbone directly below my ear with my hand angling about 45 degrees above horizontal.

Another crucial aspect of anchoring is where and how much the string touches your face. You can have the string slide right down along your nose. That's what I did as a finger shooter. Now as a release shooter, I lightly place the string at the middle or end of my nose. Make sure you always apply the same pressure from face to string. Light to no pressure is best. If you impart varying face pressure on the string, it'll bend the string and change your sight picture, causing different points of arrow impact.

Dave Johnson of Spot-Hogg Archery Products has experimented extensively with face pressure against the string and its effect on point of impact. With the aid of his "Hooter Shooter" shooting machine he was able to get tangible results. Just by pressing his face against the string he could alter the arrow's point of impact by as much as 18 to 20 inches (46 to 51 cm) at 20 yards (18 m)! He discovered the more intense the stress, whether while

hunting or shooting in a tournament, he'd try harder and thus unknowingly press his face harder against the string. It caused him fits with erratic arrow groups until he figured it out. He discovered any variation of pressure on the bowstring, whether it be from the cheek, nose, chin or chest, will change where the arrows impact. He suggests not touching the string at all.

Releasing

Most bowhunters who switch to a trigger release from finger shooting usually achieve immediately improved accuracy and feel good about their new purchase. Unfortunately, very few learn to shoot a release aid properly from the start. Most archers use some type of controlled punch to trigger the release. This works quite well for some time. Yet, sooner or later, they struggle with getting the sight pin on the target and keeping it there. They'll find themselves flinching, gunching or mashing the trigger as the pin gets close to the spot they so desperately hope to hit. For some it gets so bad they end up pushing the bow at the last instant to try to get the sight on target.

This is called target panic or buck fever, which is covered in Chapter 17, The Mental Aspects of Bowhunting. For now just realize the conscious mind can only do one chore at a time. With archery, that one conscious thing must be aiming. All other aspects of the shot sequence—including arrow release—must occur on a subconscious level. If you are thinking about and anticipating when to snap the trigger, you can't be aiming, right?

Here's how to release the arrow on a subconscious level:

• Get so close to a safe backstop that you don't have to worry about where the arrow goes.

• Step by step, think about every phase of your shooting form litany.

• After each step is addressed, let it become subconscious.

• With your eyes closed, come to full draw. Once you're anchored, pretend your trigger finger is an unmovable metal hook that you'll place on the release trigger.

• Imagine you have a steel cable attached to the static hook that runs up to the elbow, around the back of the upper arm and connects to the scapula on your right shoulder (for right-handed shooters).

•With eyes still closed, start moving your cable-like elbow and right shoulder back as if you are trying to squeeze an apple between your shoulder blades. Remember not to move your trigger finger. Let the elbow and back movement tighten your finger on the trigger. Eventually the bowstring will pull taut against the wall of the cam's draw cycle and give no more.

• Keep pulling through until the shot goes off.

Initially, it'll take up to 20 or more seconds to bring the shot to fruition. It might even scare you when the bow goes off. That's normal. At this point you are learning to use back tension to trigger the bow with a surprise release—not moving your finger. With enough blind practice, perhaps as much as 2,000 shots, it'll become muscle memory and a natural part of your shooting form. You'll know you're doing it right when you can comfortably draw, anchor, close eyes and pull through the shot to a surprise release in between five and eight seconds and it feels good doing it.

The next phase is to shoot with eyes open but no sight and no target. You are just getting the feel and visual aspect of a surprise release with eyes open. Once you feel comfortable with this, put your sight on the bow. Then, while standing very close to backstop, say 5 or 6 feet (1.5 or 1.8 m), shoot at an exaggerated bull's-eye target. An 8-inch (20-cm) paper plate works well. You can hardly miss a paper plate at 5 feet. The idea is to let the sight pin float around the center of the plate. You are learning to trust that you don't have to hold perfectly steady to hit in the center.

The key to this whole process is to consciously start the pulling by giving it some command. I use "start the motor." Then switch the conscious mind back to aiming and let muscle memory release the arrow. As you become more comfortable with releasing the arrow via back tension, slowly move back from the target and reduce the size of the aiming spot. If at any point you start getting too shaky to hold on the spot or it takes too long to pull through the shot, move closer and repeat the process.

Learning to shoot with back tension is a long-term project and it can't be rushed or mastered the week before deer season. I started shooting in the basement with eyes closed in March. I never shot an arrow farther than 8 yards (7 m) until June. Then, I shot at 20 yards (18 m) or less until I'd mastered the technique. It was mid-July before I started shooting at longer yardages. By September, I was consistently shooting softball-sized groups or smaller at 60 yards (55 m)—with fixed-blade broadheads!

I did not invent this method of shooting or the learning process. I've received advice from several excellent coaches, most notably, Randy Ulmer and Bernie Pellerite.

Follow-Through

When shooting with a release the follow-through is very similar to finger shooting. The relaxed trigger hand, upon surprise release, should snap straight back and touch the end of the shoulder. The bow should gently fall straight forward.

Be sure not to collapse the bow arm—it must stay at shooting height until the arrow impacts the intended target. The farther the target the more important this becomes. Don't pull through the shot to trigger the release, pull through the shot to touch fingers to the tip of the shoulder. It's called committing to the conclusion of the shot sequence.

RELEASE AIDS AND SAFETY

When choosing a mechanical release aid, keep your safety and that of others in mind. You may want to consider a release aid with some type of safety mechanism—it's reassuring. First, it'll keep the release from firing prematurely. If you accidentally bump the trigger while drawing, you'll smack yourself right in the face. Trust me, it hurts. Furthermore, upon accidental firing, you don't know where your arrow will end up, and that's certainly not safe.

Once, I put an arrow through my basement window when a release aid went off unexpectedly. Luckily, all was fine except a bruised nose, a broken window and considerable embarrassment. A release aid with a safety would have prevented all of that.

Also, regardless of whether your release has a safety mechanism, always keep your finger behind the trigger or on top of the release body while drawing. Only put your finger on the trigger when you are ready to shoot. If you make this a conscious part of your shot sequence in practice, this "safety" will occur naturally when hunting.

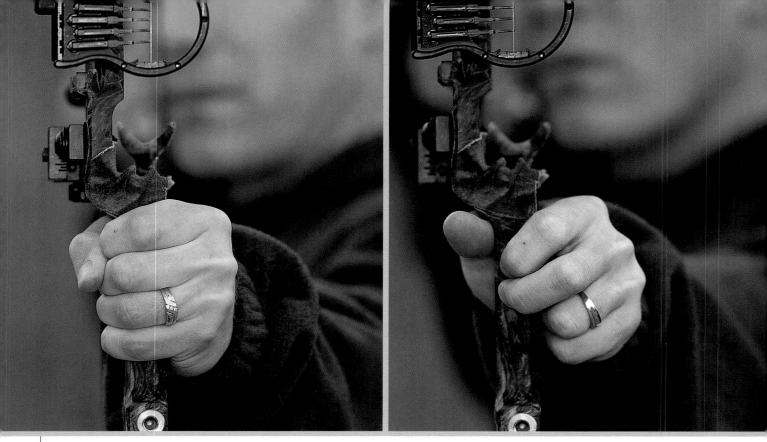

A tight, "death grip" hand hold on the bow (left) produces uneven torque and dramatically reduces accuracy. A relaxed bow hand (right) is easy to repeat and allows the bow to shoot the shot—crucial aspects to pinpoint accuracy.

CHAPTER NINE

Understanding Bow Torque

The simple textbook definition of torque is "twisting or wrenching effect." As it applies to shooting a bow, if your hand is not placed properly on the handle and the bow kicks in any manner other than straight forward upon the shot, you are torquing the bow. Too short or, more likely, too long of a draw length can cause bow torque. But usually, torque occurs from grabbing and holding the bow incorrectly. Remember, the bow—not the archer—is supposed to shoot the shot. If your bow hand is doing anything more than providing a relaxed cradle for the bow at full draw, you are reducing your accuracy potential.

Hand Position

For the most consistent results, you must discover a hand position that is relaxed, comfortable and, most important, easy to duplicate shot after shot. Some people have short, thick hands while others have long, slender hands. Additionally every bow company makes bow handles a little differently. So, there is no universal hand placement for all archers. However, there are some proven guidelines to steer you in the right direction.

Take a look at your bow hand. Notice what is commonly called the "lifeline" in the palm. This

58

UNDERSTANDING BOW TORQUE

line basically divides the major muscles in your hand and forms a natural crease in which to place the bow handle. Instead of grabbing the bow, try adding this step to your shot sequence: After nocking the arrow and placing the finger tab or release on the string, dangle the weight of the bow from your drawing hand/release. Then, gently pull the bow back up into the lifeline crease of your bow hand. Make sure the thumb is completely relaxed. You can even tuck two or three fingers so your knuckles are gently touching the side of the bow handle. Then gently place just the tip of your index finger or index finger and middle finger to the back of the bow. The tucked fingers keep you from torquing and the fingertips on the back of the bow provide confidence and a little security so you won't drop the bow upon release.

The bowhunter silently slipped into the woods, descented clothes and all. Shortly, he was waiting patiently in his elevated tree stand. He was vigilant for hours. Finally he relaxed and let his guard down, as so many of us do. He hung his bow on a hook instead of keeping it in his hand with a bow sling in place. Of course, Murphy's Law reared its ironic head: A dandy eight-point buck materialized in front of the unprepared hunter. When the buck paused behind a tree that blocked its vision but not the vitals, the hunter grabbed his compound bow, drew, aimed and shot the buck cleanly. As the arrow hit the deer, much to the hunter's surprise, his bow plummeted 30 feet to the ground, scattering arrows with a racket like a kid dumping Lincoln Logs on a tile floor.

"I felt kind of silly at first," said Randy Ulmer, world-class tournament archer and renowned bowhunter. "But then it dawned on me what happened. In the rush to get my bow back in my hand, I forgot to use the bow sling. The bow fell to the ground because I didn't grip my bow!"

Now that's what I call good and repeatable bow hand placement in a real hunting situation. I don't recommend everyone drop his or her bow from a tree stand but a relaxed bow hand is instrumental to consistent hunting accuracy.

Handle Choices

Contrary to what some manufacturers would have you believe, a slick, thin handle with no texture is best for repeatable hand placement. If you cup your hand in the same manner for every shot, a slick handle will automatically slide the bow hand into the handle consistently. I know tournament archers who wear a slick, fingerless glove on their bow hand so it will slide into the bow handle the same way each time. Some archers wrap the bow handle with a slick Teflon tape to ensure their hand slides into place in a repeatable fashion.

A thin handle reduces torque because there is less hand surface area contacting the bow. The less hand contacting the bow, the less likely you will torque the bow. For example, when using a screwdriver to thread a wood screw into hardwood, you naturally grab the fat handle of the screwdriver with your entire hand because it provides the most torque or twisting effect necessary to thread the screw into the wood. On the contrary, it would be extremely difficult to thread the screw into the board by only twisting the screwdriver blade between two fingers because the thin blade doesn't produce much torque.

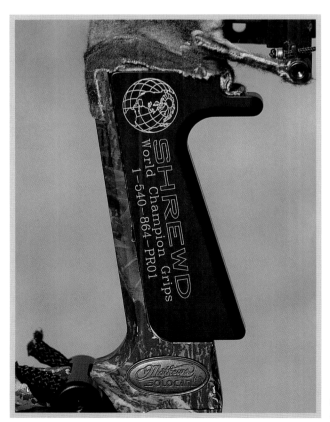

On a custom grip like this Shrewd or those made by Hicks and Loesch, the narrow throat reduces bow torque.

Many top tournament archers simply remove the handle of their bow and place their hand directly on the riser because it's thinner. Also, there are several companies that make very thin custom handles. Some have prefabricated custom handles; others will actually make a handle to fit your unique hand shape. I've even made my own thin handles, with excellent results.

Continuing this concept, if a bow handle has any texture or rubber grip, it will be more difficult to repeat hand placement. I saw this firsthand when testing my archery tackle with the Hooter Shooter shooting machine made by Spot-Hogg Archery Products. The kind folks at Spot-Hogg were helping me with some experiments for this book. We were able to get my bow to shoot the same arrow in the same hole, shot after shot with their machine. In the middle of a test, however, the arrows starting impacting differently so we sprayed the handle with WD-40 and with the slicker handle, the arrows went back to hitting in the same hole! Adhesive-backed fleece covering the riser shelf overflowed onto the bow handle. That fleece texture caused the machine to hold the bow differently and, thus, changed the point of impact.

If a small piece of fleece can make an arrow impact several inches (centimeters) differently at 20 yards (18 m) in laboratory conditions, just think what a rubber grip and a textured glove on an excited bowhunter's hand could do to the arrow's point of impact in the field!

Grip Options

For some reason, many archers put a stranglehold on the bow handle—as if they're afraid the bow is going to fly away upon releasing the arrow. This "death grip" is a surefire way to lessen accuracy and shooting confidence. I recommend using a wrist strap that's tight enough to provide the mental security that you won't drop the bow. But don't wear it so tight that it causes torque. About 1 inch (2.5 cm) of slack on the wrist strap is a good place to start. That's the best way to eliminate the death grip ailment.

Choosing a compound bow with a more parallel limb design that reduces the recoil, or installing a good stabilizer to reduce bow jump upon release will help, too.

Somewhere along your ever-winding path of archery knowledge, someone probably told you to shoot with an open hand and not to grab the bow. So you tried it. Unfortunately, the bow probably jumped in your hand. It maybe even have hit the floor at the archery shop in an embarrassing racket. So you've now got the "handle-grabbing" malady. You shoot with an open hand but, upon the release, you quickly close your hand to keep the bow from getting away. Most likely, you anticipate the explosion of the shot and start to grab before the arrow has cleared the bow. This reduces accuracy because it's nearly impossible to do this exactly the same way with every shot. In essence, when trying not to grab the bow, you end up grabbing it more radically!

As with the death grip, shooting a low-recoil bow, installing a wrist strap, getting a surprise release and an improved follow-through are the antidotes for the handle-grabbing disease. If you are anticipating the release so you can grab the bow, you are not concentrating on aiming. If you shoot with a surprise release, you don't know when the bow is going off so you don't know when to grab.

Also, shooting with eyes closed and intentionally concentrating on the follow-through phase of the shot will help. Get close to the backstop, relax, let the bow shoot the shot, and don't move your bow hand until well after the arrow impacts the target. Once you're in the habit of not grabbing the handle, shooting at long range will force you to improve follow-through as well.

Hand Tension

A relaxed hand is much easier to duplicate than a tense hand. While at full draw, have someone actually try to wriggle the thumb and fingers of your bow hand. If they don't move easily, you should lighten up and relax your bow hand.

Another way to check for tension is to look at your bow hand while at full draw. If you see bunched-up or severely wrinkled skin from holding the bow, a different hand position and a more relaxed hand are in order.

The shape of your arrow group patterns is another indicator that you may be torquing the bow. If your arrows spray across the target in a horizontal fashion, you may be putting too much thumb and palm pressure on the bow or twisting your fingers around the handle too much. If your arrows are grouping in a more vertical fashion, you are probably altering your wrist position from shot to shot.

If your arrows tend to group in a horizontal manner like this, you may be inadvertently altering your thumb and palm pressure on the bow handle, from shot to shot.

Wrist Position

Changing your wrist from a high to medium to low position can change the arrow's point of impact at 20 yards (18 m) by 5 to 8 inches (13 to 20 cm)! If you don't believe me, try shooting with different wrist positions but keeping the sight settings the same. Your arrow will fly to a different point of impact—I promise.

In general, a high wrist position takes a lot of strength and is hard to duplicate. A medium wrist is better and easier to repeat. A low wrist position allows the hand and wrist bones to line up with the arm bones for a consistent, relaxed bow hand.

Experimenting

In the long run, dedicating a couple afternoons to experimenting with hand and wrist positions of the bow hand is time well spent. Try putting Vaseline, talc or cooking oil on your bow hand and the handle. The slickness will make your hand slip into the handle the same way every time.

Then, install a long stabilizer made for target shooting or tape an arrow to your short hunting stabilizer. Shoot at close range and watch which way the stabilizer kicks. If it kicks upward you are putting too much palm heel pressure on the handle. If the stabilizer kicks downward, you are putting too much tension on the top of the handle. For a right-handed archer, if the stabilizer kicks left, you're pushing too hard with the thumb side of the hand. And, if it kicks right, you have too much tension on the finger side of the bow hand.

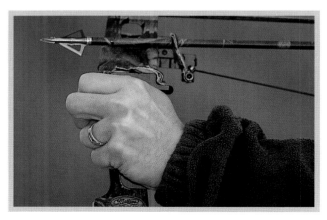

Here are examples of high (top), medium (middle) and low (bottom) wrist positions with two fingers tucked for accurate shooting. Of the three, the high wrist is most difficult to duplicate. A medium to low wrist will usually produce the best results.

Bowhunter Frank Jirik shooting with eyes closed to "feel" proper shooting form.

CHAPTER TEN

Preseason Shooting Preparation

Many bowhunters are like electricity. They take the path of least resistance. Rarely is this easy route the best conduit for success, but preseason preparation is. I promise you, hunters who consistently hang their tags on big-racked bucks are shooters who've paid their dues at the practice range–long before opening day.

The following is an excellent preseason warm-up routine. If you are serious about being prepared, starting six months prior to hunting season is none too soon.

Equipment Selection

Early to mid-winter is the time to try any number of new things, such as buy a new bow, switch from aluminum arrows to carbon, upgrade your release, try a new broadhead, change to a fall-away arrow rest. Even if you stick with your tried-and-true bowhunting rig, dig it out of the closet, dust it off and begin some preseason preparation.

When you start early, there's no rush. If you miss a day or two now, it's no big deal–not so when

PRESEASON SHOOTING PREPARATION

you've waited until the last week before hunting season. This long-term process allows you to enjoy preseason preparation without haste or pressure, and to have the time to make adjustments.

First, do a thorough inspection. Replace any worn parts. If needed, replace the string and bus cables in tandem. It usually takes about 200 shots to "break in" new strings. And, it'll take a lot more shooting than that to re-tone your shooting muscles. Don't worry too much about arrow flight and tuning just yet. Work on your shooting form first.

Shooting by Feel

Shooting with your eyes closed and learning to feel what a good shot feels like with proper form may seem unorthodox at first, but it's the best method to improve concentration and shooting form without worrying about accuracy. Unfortunately, most "electric" bowhunters head straight to the target range and are so consumed by results, they forget about number one—shooting form. Without proper shooting form, achieving consistently accurate arrow flight is impossible. (For a reminder on good shooting form, review Chapter 7.)

Shooting by feel with your eyes closed begins by shooting just a few yards (meters) from a large target backstop. Get comfortable; raise the bow to shooting height to make sure the blind shot will safely hit the backstop. Then, before drawing, close your eyes. With eyes shut, draw the bow, feel the anchor and smoothly release the arrow. Concentrate only on shooting form. Remember, a few perfectly executed shots are more beneficial, especially early on, than dozens of haphazard attempts.

Even after forty-one years of archery experience, I frequently shoot some "blind" practice. This may seem boring but it helps more than you can imagine. One, it's a good way to start toning shooting muscles. Two, blind practice greatly improves muscle memory so you are repeating each step of your shot sequence consistently.

When you can't see the target, you don't worry about aiming. Instead, you'll find yourself in a trance-like state that allows the drawing of the bow and release of the arrow to become something you simply feel—a smooth, easy motion that fosters accurate shooting. Additionally, this shooting-by-feel method helps improve follow-through because you are not all caught up in seeing where the arrow hits.

Blind practice is also a valuable tool during the hunting season when you feel something is not right with your shooting. Shoot blind for at least a few days—two or three weeks would be better. This is especially true if you are learning to shoot with back tension instead of punching, switching to a release aid for the first time or trying a different style of release aid.

Try shooting blind—you'll be amazed at how much it can improve your overall shooting ability.

Bow Tuning

Now that you have broken-in your new string and bus cable and toned your shooting muscles, you can begin the tuning process. Remember that without consistent shooting form, you can't make arrow rest or nock set adjustments with any degree of success. Also, keep in mind that each change in your bow-and-arrow setup, no matter how small, may affect how arrows fly and where they impact—especially with broadheads.

Regardless of whether you are shooting a new rig or your dusty, trusty old bow, tune the arrow flight now. One of the best ways to tune arrow flight is to shoot through paper. Like deer tracks in the snow, you can read the signs. The tears tell you what adjustments are needed.

Another excellent method of tuning is the bare-shaft test. (See Chapter 14 for a complete explanation of bow tuning.) Make sure you shoot your bow during the tuning process. It doesn't mean diddly if your bow shoots clean arrow flight for a pro-shop clerk or your buddy.

With a well-tuned bow, compound or traditional, you'll improve accuracy and confidence much faster. For me, the bottom line in bow tuning is, I can accept my innate human errors. However, I want quality equipment to work as intended. That way, if an arrow does go askew, there's only one problem—the jerk behind the trigger.

Zeroing-In

The next step is to sight-in. This process may take several sessions before your sight pins are properly set. The worst thing you can do is force yourself into a hurried, one-session sight-in. Fatigue and frustration will surely set in and your whole training regimen will backslide. Be patient during the early stages. Don't rush anything; build up to it.

I set my 20- and 30-yard (18- and 27-m) pins the first day and then 40s (36 m) and 50s (45.5 m) the second day. Later, when I'm really dialed in, I'll set my 60-yard (55-m) pin. At first, the pins may not be set exactly right, but they're close. Several days later, when my shooting muscles are fresh and I'm able to concentrate, I shoot a few close-up, eyes-closed arrows. Then I try to precisely set each pin. I can usually get dialed-in within a few sessions.

A month or so before hunting season, I follow the same procedure after replacing field tips with broadheads. Even with a well-tuned bow, broadheads may impact differently from field tips but they should still group well. Since I've switched to a fall-away arrow rest, however, I've had all styles of broadheads and field tips group to the same point of impact. Remember, having bow sights set perfectly for broadheads—not field tips—before heading into the deer woods provides confidence well worth the time and cost of a few practice broadheads.

Practice Distances

Initial practice sessions should be limited to short-distance shooting of 10 to 30 yards (9 to 27 m). Take your time with each shot, concentrate on the spot yet try to remain as relaxed as possible while at full draw. Try to shoot the best groups you can. Remember, it's always better to shoot fewer "quality" arrows before your shooting form begins to falter than to shoot more shots when you're fatigued.

Once you become deadly up close, move back and begin adding 40-yard (36-m), 50-yard (45.5-m) and longer shots to your practice regimen. This is very important even for tree stand whitetail hunters who may never take a shot longer than 25 yards (23 m).

The reason is simple: Consistently making longer shots requires more concentration, better shooting form and a smoother release. Everything has to be just right. At first, you'll see arrow groups resembling a shotgun pattern. But if you've paid your dues with blind practice and have good form and a well-tuned bow, your groups will tighten up. And then, when you move into more realistic hunting distances, you'll be amazed at how easy it is to place arrow after arrow inside the 10-ring on a 3-D target.

Once I'm really dialed-in, I reverse my shooting regimen. I start out shooting the longer distances first. Then, as I get tired, I move closer. This way, I almost always shoot good groups at all yardages. When I do that, shooting confidence soars.

Make Practice Fun

Target practice using bull's-eye targets set at known distances is essential to getting sighted-in, refining shooting form and gaining both the physical ability and confidence to make the shot. As the hunting season gets closer, it's time to try new games that both simulate bowhunting situations, and help you shoot under the kinds of pressure that arise when a deer walks into view.

• Archery leagues are an excellent year-round way to stay sharp, both mentally and physically. By shooting in a weekly league, you will keep your equipment in tip-top shape, bow-shooting muscles toned and aiming skills sharp. Competitive league shooting also provides pressure to succeed. It's not the same pressure you feel when a big buck saunters by, but it's similar. If you can handle tournament pressure, it may help you handle hunting pressure. Your local archery club or pro shop should have information on nearby league shooting.

• Interactive video archery is another fun and excellent form of practice for the bowhunter. Video archery features a large, impact-sensitive screen upon which a video of an animal is played. The bowhunter then shoots blunt-tipped arrows right at the screen. With the magic of technology, it shows you where the arrow would have struck a live animal and what the results of that hit would be. Video archery leagues are available both locally and nationally. They are an exciting and fun way to practice inside when the weather is too hot, cold or wet to enjoy archery outside.

If arrows impact high left, move the pin high and left—always "chase" the arrow with the pin.

• Another very popular way to practice is 3-D target shooting. Most bowhunting clubs have their own life-size 3-D targets and ranges. You can practice not at bull's-eye targets set at known distances, but instead at life-size animal replicas placed at unmarked yardages. This is some of the most realistic preseason practice a bowhunter can experience. I've had my best autumns of bowhunting success after a full summer of 3-D competition. Give it a try.

• You may want to try a friendly, yet competitive, game of follow-the-leader. Either on an established 3-D range or a safe wood lot, have one person pick the distance, angle and target. That person kneels down and shoots—often at weird angles and through holes in the brush. Others follow suit to see who can judge yardage and shoot the best.

• You can even play archery golf or mimic dart games. It takes some real estate and time to set up a course but when several people pitch in, the work is tolerable and it makes for some great practice.

Remember, archery enthusiasm can be like a burning ember. In the company of others it can burn bright and hot, but alone it can cool off and burn out. Get involved with your local and state bowhunting organizations—give back to the sport you love.

Regardless of which practice games you choose, start out shooting at bull's-eye targets and graduate to animal targets prior to the hunt. Learning to pick and concentrate on a small spot on a live animal's side is one of the hardest things to do while hunting. In my opinion, not picking a spot is the most significant cause of misses or, worse yet, bad hits. Thus, for the last few weeks before the season, only shoot at animal targets without an aiming spot. This will get you used to picking your own spot come hunting season.

Training Techniques

As bowhunting season approaches, it's time for what I call "species-specific" practice. All competitive athletes, such as Olympic track stars, pro golfers, competitive skiers, practice the specific movements and skills needed to succeed in their sport. This type of practice works for bowhunters, too. To maximize the positive effects of this training, try to duplicate the conditions you'll be hunting in as closely as possible.

Probably most of your hunting is from a tree stand set about 18 feet (5.5 m) high. The brush is thick enough that most shot opportunities will be less than 30 yards (27 m). For species-specific practice,

place a tree stand 18 feet high and scatter several targets around it between 10 and 30 yards (9 and 27 m) away. Plastic, gallon (3-liter) milk jugs partially filled with sand work well for this. Then don your hunting clothes and climb up. Put on your safety harness, hang your bow as you do when hunting, sit down and get comfortable. There's no rush—you're simulating a real bow hunt.

Pick a target, reach slowly for your bow, draw, aim and shoot. Hang the bow back up, take your time, pick another target, repeat the process. This may seem tedious but it simulates the kinds of shots you'll be taking come fall. And it forces you to go through your mental pre-shot checklist. Most quirks, such as string slap on your coat sleeve or a bow limb clanking on the tree stand, should become apparent during this species-specific practice.

For example, before I went on my musk ox hunt, I donned all my arctic clothing and shot my bow. Every time I did this, the bulky clothes altered my shooting form just enough to change my arrows' point of impact. I re-sighted my bow to hit spot-on when wearing heavy clothes. When I got my chance at a near–Boone and Crockett–class musk-ox bull, I made the shot with confidence. Without the species-specific practice, who knows what might have happened?

In addition, species-specific practice should include appropriate physical fitness and anatomy study of your target species. From firsthand experience, I've learned a few details: A mountain goat's vitals are more underneath its massive front shoulders than behind it. A bear's heart and lungs are more compact, lower and farther forward than a deer's. A moose's liver extends beyond mid-body. The point is, learn about your target animal before the hunt.

Well before the hunt, Lon became familiar with his bow rig and the bulky clothes needed to hunt musk ox in cold weather.

Rich Eckles prepares to shoot while his twin brother, Rob, verifies distance with a laser range finder.

CHAPTER ELEVEN

Estimating Yardage

The most common reason bowhunters miss their quarry? The arching trajectory of an arrow couples with misjudging the distance to a target animal. For example:

Years ago, while hunting Columbian black-tailed deer in the mountains of northern California, my buddy, South Cox, and I glassed up a fabulous buck with tall, fuzzy antlers. His Boone and Crockett–class rack sported six tines on each side. The deer was feeding in a lush green valley with a cool stream trickling down the center. Since I spotted him first, it was my stalk.

After carefully descending 600 feet (183 m) in elevation and sneaking across the valley floor like a mountain lion, the stalk started to gel. I had plenty of brush for cover and the buck was feeding my way. Shortly, the deer moved out into an open area near the stream. From a kneeling position, I estimated the distance at 43 yards (39 m). I cut a good arrow, but the buck scrambled off unscathed. Upon stepping-off the distance, I learned he was actually 47 yards (43 m) away. My arrow had flown just below his brisket.

Eyeballing Distance

There are several tricks a bowhunter can use to improve his or her range estimation skills. First, rehearse yardage estimation just like shooting practice—with diligence. Start out by "calibrating" your eye at the practice range with known distances. Really study the ground distance between you and the 20-yard (18-m) target, then the 30-yard (27-m) target, etc. Next, practice pacing off the distance to the backstops to gauge your step to 1-yard (1-m) strides. Once you've learned to walk with incremental paces, you can practice range estimation just about anywhere. Even better is verifying your range estimation with the reading of a quality laser range finder.

When walking down the street, look at an object, say a light post, and guess how far away it is. Then pace off the distance to see how close you "guessed." Continually doing this will sharpen your distance-judging abilities. Don't be disappointed if you're off by several yards (meters). It takes time to improve this skill. Always try to estimate to the exact yardage. A ballpark distance, give or take 5 yards (4.5 m), will not be effective due to the arching trajectory of your arrow.

Leap-Frog Method

Everyone has his or her own method of judging yardage. Here's what I do: First, I try to disregard the animal's size and only look at the gap of real estate between the target animal and me. The reason for disregarding animal size is simple—game animals are not created equally. For instance, not every whitetail buck will have the same body thickness. And, if you've never been around moose, when that first bull steps out, he'll appear so large you'll likely think he's 30 yards (27 m) away when he may actually be closer to 50 yards (45.5 m).

My second step is to mentally and visually estimate what I believe is 20 yards (18 m). Then I visually "leap frog" in 20-yard increments until I get to my subject.

Third is my "verification" step. I try to guess half the distance between the target animal and me. Once I've estimated that distance, I multiply by two and compare that yardage estimation with the distance I obtained from the second step, the 20-yard method.

I killed a dandy bull caribou while hunting in the mighty Alaska Range west of Fairbanks, AK, using the leap-frog and half-the-distance methods.

After twelve hours of crawling and chasing, I finally got a break. It was late evening and the two bull caribou started to mill around and feed. They had been resting in an unapproachable basin for most of the afternoon. Their feeding path led them directly below a steep, stair-step-type ridge.

I sprinted around and above them. My timing was perfect. When I peeked over the ridge the bulls were contentedly munching on lichens in the soft tundra below. Quickly, I visually leap-frogged down the mountain. I thought to myself, "That boulder appears to be 20 yards [18 m]. That blueberry bush is another 20 yards and the caribou are about 5 yards [4.5 m] beyond that." Then I concluded, "Okay, the swale in the tundra looks about halfway to the bulls, and that seems about 23 yards [21 m] away." So I came to 45 yards [42 m] on the first guess and 46 [42 m] on the second. "If I subtract a few yards for the steep downhill angle, I should shoot for 40 yards [36 m]."

Shortly after that range estimation, I was happily but hurriedly processing the caribou to beat the impending darkness.

By employing the visual leap-frog method of range estimation, Lon killed this Pope and Young–class barren-ground caribou bull at approximately 45 yards.

You can further calibrate your eye by practicing these methods on a 3-D animal target course. First, give it your best estimation, then confirm it with a laser range finder.

Pin Gap Method

Another way to help judge distance is by using your bow's sight pins as a crude range finder. Let's say you set sight pins so arrows hit at 20, 30 and 40 yards (18, 27 and 36 m). The gaps between the pins become your measuring sticks. For example, on my current bow the 20- to 30-yard pin gap is literally 3/16 inch (4.8 mm) and another 3/16 inch between 30 and 40. Thus, when comparing the gap between those pins to a downrange object, I can estimate the yardage: When I come to full draw and size-up an object, I know the space between my 20- and 40-yard pins will span a vertical distance of 20 inches (51 cm) at 40 yards (36 m). That's about the same back-to-brisket height of a whitetail.

Of course, this method varies depending on the specific trajectory of your arrows. The easiest way to determine this is to shoot at 40 yards while aiming with your 20- and 30-yard pins. Next, measure how many inches (centimeters) low your arrows impacted on the target. Not only will this evaluation give you another tool for range estimation, it'll clearly illustrate just how much arching trajectory occurs with your hunting rig.

You can apply this method to actual hunting scenarios. Although deer are not always the same size, 20 inches is about the depth of an average whitetail from back to brisket. For example, if a deer walks into my shooting lane, I know the deer is about 40 yards away. When at full draw, my 20-yard pin is even with the buck's back and my 40-yard pin is even with his brisket. If both 20-yard and 40-yard pins are well within the animal's depth, I'm closer than 30 yards. If his body fits between the 20- and 30-yard pins he's more like 50 yards (45.5 m) away.

Remember, a much larger or smaller deer, or shooting a bow with different trajectory/pin gap than my setup will alter these calculations. It's a crude range finder but can be effective in a pinch.

Detail Method

One other range estimation method is to notice what details of your target animal you can clearly see. Everyone's vision is different so it's something you have to develop on your own.

For example, at 30 yards (27 m) and closer, you can see individual hairs on a buck. At 40 (36 m), you can see texture and muscle definition but not individual hair. At 50 yards (45.5 m), you start losing all detail in the animal's pelage and can only visualize major muscle groups like the hindquarter and front shoulder.

If you employ this method, beware of changing light conditions. On a sunny day, you're likely to see more detail at longer distances than on an overcast or rainy day.

The best way to improve this skill is going to a zoo or game farm, with laser range finder in tow, then guess and verify, guess and verify.

For the Tree Stand Hunter

If you frequently hunt from the same tree stand, either step off yardage to likely shooting lanes or employ a laser range finder. You can either use descented flagging material or sticks-turned-yardage-markers poked into the ground at known distances. Of the two, I prefer using natural objects instead of flagging. The following hunting experience taught me why.

One time my friend and hunting partner, Dan McKinley, placed orange flagging on some wheat stubble exactly 30 yards (27 m) from his stand. Then, one evening, a mature doe wandered by and ate the flagging! Shortly after his yardage marker was consumed and the doe had moved on, a Boone and Crockett–class buck sauntered into the field. With no distance reference across the nondescript sea of wheat, estimating yardage was extremely difficult. Unfortunately, Dan missed the shot.

During off-hours, bowhunters often practice judging yardage and picking a spot on life-size 3-D animal targets.

Using Range Finders

The birth of laser range finders has fueled controversy among the bowhunting ranks. Traditionalists may say laser range finders are for sissies—real bowhunters don't need to be told the yardage. High-tech advocates may be staunch supporters, believing that no one could discredit a bowhunter using a device that greatly improves the odds of making a humane kill. Regardless of what equipment you choose, laser range finders have several advantages and a few hindrances.

Advantages

First and foremost, a properly used and accurate laser range finder can increase shooting confidence substantially. Studies have proven most people are inadequate at judging yardage, especially past 30 yards (27 m). With a range finder, the hunter knows the exact distance and can then concentrate on executing the shot. A hunter who is guessing yardage may be thinking about the accuracy of the "guess" instead of aiming. Undoubtedly, shot placement will suffer. Changing your mind on yardage while at full draw erodes confidence like a flash flood washing away a sand dune. If you think you are going to miss, you will. Knowing the distance gives a bowhunter a huge mental edge.

Even fast arrows only diminish range estimation errors by a few inches (centimeters). And there's usually a degradation of accuracy in hunting conditions when shooting a super-fast arrow. So, if the faster bow sprays arrow groups wider than it decreases trajectory, you've defeated the purpose. It would be much better to shoot a slower, more consistently accurate arrow while employing a

Josh Pape uses a Bushnell Scout laser range finder from inside a Double Bull ground blind.

range finder. That's what I do. My typical hunting setup usually lobs arrows at 240 fps (73 mps).

Here's an example of just how proficient of a yardage guesser you must be in a hunting situation without the aid of a laser range finder. An archer shooting at a deer with a pie-plate-size kill zone from 50 yards (45.5 m) away with an arrow leaving the bow at 280 fps (85 mps) would have to judge the distance to the animal no closer than 46.1 yards (41.9 m) and no farther than 53.4 yards (48.6) to make a clean kill. If the hunter misjudges yardage more than that, whether long or short, he'll miss. Thus, the inherent arc of even a fast arrow requires the skill to judge yardage to within an average of plus-or-minus 3 yards (2.7 m).

There's another tactical hunting advantage to using a laser range finder. From afar, you can range to the animal, say 100 yards (91 m), and then range to a landmark such as the boulder you intend to shoot from. By subtracting the distance from your present location to the rock, say 80 yards (73 m), you'll know to shoot for 20 yards (18 m) once you've reached your boulder. This tactic eliminates the potential game-spooking movement necessary to operate a laser range finder. Keep in mind, the closer you get, the more likely your quarry will pick up any movement.

Also, if the stalk falls apart, you can range from your "got-busted" location to the deer's bed to determine how close you came to bringing the stalk to fruition. Saying, "I got 73 yards (66 m) from the buck before he blazed out of there" is cannon fodder for self-confidence.

Furthermore, if you are shooting at game in steep country and there's a tree towering up near your quarry, you can range to the tree across the level/horizontal distance and shoot for that yardage without having to be a geometry major.

In my opinion, these confidence-building factors make a laser range finder worth the purchase price and far outweigh their limitations.

Disadvantages

Using a range finder increases the need for movement. Frequently, just drawing the bow in the presence of game is challenging enough. Grabbing, raising the device to your eye and putting it away may be too much movement and might squelch a shot opportunity. Additionally, the extra time needed to use a range finder may cost you a shot, as I once found out.

I waited hours for a group of caribou to feed over a ridge. When the herd bull, lagging behind the cows, finally grazed out of sight, I sprinted up and over the hill.

By the time I'd covered the half mile (0.8 km), all the "bou" were down in the next flat, except the bull. When I crept over the rise I caught him quartering away, head down and feeding. By the time I pulled out the ranger finder, used it, put it away and came to full draw, the bull trotted down the hill to join his harem. Had I relied on my own range estimation skills I probably would have tagged that bull. He was only 27 yards (24.5 m) away. I'd become so reliant on the range finder, I didn't even think about estimating yardage the old-fashioned way.

Using a laser range finder when shooting uphill and downhill requires a solid knowledge of geometry. Remember, when shooting at steep angles, the arrow is only affected by gravity across the level distance, not the longer, angled yardage. (See Chapter 18 for more information on shooting at steep angles.)

Even though I'm acutely aware of the thought process of shooting at steep angles, I've missed animals because of poor triangulation. This triangulation theory can affect yardage on flat ground, too.

On another caribou hunt, I had a beautiful bull wander right into my ambush. Other than the grass mogul I was hunkered behind, it was open tundra. I ranged off the only rock in his path, which was at a steep angle to my right. The range finder indicated the small boulder was 45 yards (41 m) away. The bull walked right by the rock and continued on a fairly straight course. When the bull was slightly past me, I drew my bow. He stopped. I remember placing the 40-yard (36-m) pin right at the top of his back so the arrow would drop into the vitals for the "range finder's 45 yards." I cut an excellent shot. The arrow zipped through the hair on the bull's back— within an inch (2.5 cm) of where my 40-yard (36-m) pin was aimed. As the bull trotted off, I realized my error. It was 45 yards (41 m) to the rock at about a 70-degree angle. When the bull walked in front of me he was only about 40 yards away. Aiming 5 yards (4.5 m) off with a 230-fps (70-mps) arrow doesn't get the job done!

When you know the distance to a target animal, you can shoot with more confidence and concentrate on picking a spot and aiming without being distracted with guessing yardage.

Another problem I've experienced with laser range finders is their literacy. This electronic device cannot discern what you want it to range. You may think you're ranging off the white hump of a mountain goat's back when in reality the range finder is reading off a wisp of tan grass 6 yards (5.5 m) closer. Does that example sound too specific to be just an example? Absolutely—it happened to me!

Finally, I feel the biggest drawback to laser range finders is the temptation to take shots beyond your personal effective range. Just because you know that antelope is 76 yards (69 m) away doesn't mean you should attempt the shot. Personal shooting abilities, wind, alertness of the game and many other factors affect such decisions. To maintain ethics and integrity, we must know our shooting skills and stick well within those limits. (See Chapter 15, Effective Shooting Range, for more on this topic.)

America's conservation pioneer Aldo Leopold said it best, "A peculiar virtue in wildlife ethics is that the hunter ordinarily has no gallery to applaud or disapprove of his conduct. Whatever his acts, they are dictated by his own conscience, rather than by a mob of onlookers. It is difficult to exaggerate the importance of this fact."

The bottom line is that any modern arrow still has an arching trajectory and thus getting close and knowing the distance to your quarry are the keys to accurate shooting.

Correy Mathews uses a compound bow and mechanical release during a winter 3-D shoot.

CHAPTER TWELVE

3-D Shooting

Shooting at three-dimensional, life-size animal targets may be the best practice for the bowhunter—if you have the right mindset. That mindset should be to use the same archery tackle you intend to hunt with and not worry about winning tournaments. I believe 3-D shooting has gone the same direction as retriever field trials. Initially, field trials were set up to test a hunting dog's abilities in mock, yet lifelike, hunting conditions. Nowadays, with heated competition, money and prestige associated with field-trial dogs, the tasks expected of our canine friends go way beyond the skills necessary to retrieve a mallard from a pond.

Similar to field trials for dogs, I believe 3-D shooting was originally designed to help bowhunters improve their range estimation skills and shooting proficiency—to make them better bowhunters. In short order, 3-D shooting has become hyper-competitive, prestigious and, in some cases, a high-dollar event. The bows have become flatter shooting and targets are shot at longer distances. Also, a small 12-point scoring ring has been added to separate pinpoint shooters from the rest of us.

In my opinion, the best bow and arrow setup for competing on the 3-D course is not necessarily the same equipment I'd choose for hunting. For example, the best 3-D shooters are zipping light arrows

(5 grains/0.32 g) of arrow weight per pound/kg of draw weight) downrange at 280 fps (80 mps) or faster. Most bowhunters are shooting a minimum of 5 to 8 grains (0.32 to 0.52 g) per pound (0.45 kg) of draw weight at 250 fps (76 mps) or less. The hunting trend is leaning toward the faster, lighter arrow also.

Bowhunting and 3-D shooting have similar, yet not exactly the same, goals. The bowhunter must correctly place the arrow in the animal's vitals for a quick harvest—by shooting a razor-sharp broadhead, with adequate kinetic energy to get full penetration from a quiet-shooting bow. Furthermore, the hunter may or may not know the yardage to the target, which depends on the type of hunting and whether a laser range finder is employed. The 3-D shooter's goal is to shoot high scores, regardless of angle, at unknown distances with no concern for bow noise, broadhead flight or penetration. As one 3-D shooter told me, "Speed is everything." True, a flatter trajectory helps in range estimation errors. However, for both 3-D shooting and hunting, consistent form, good range estimation skills and a forgiving bow are more important factors than uncontrollably fast arrow speed.

The results of a bitterly cold 3-D shoot I once competed in were a good example.

It was a nippy –4˚F (–20˚C), yet forty-seven hardy Alaskans showed up to compete. I was shooting a long axle-to-axle, high-brace-height, finger-shooting bow at the time. It was set up for hunting with 500-grain (32.40-g) aluminum arrows flying 213 fps (65 mps). This is a far cry from what would be considered a competitive 3-D rig. However, this was a very forgiving bow, and that translated into consistent accuracy. At the end of the day, I had the highest score of all competitors, including the mechanical-release shooters with the fast arrows.

Three factors contributed to the outcome: good range estimation, consistent shooting form and a forgiving bow. The first two factors need no explanation; I believe the more forgiving bow made the real difference. Remember, it was really cold that day. Hands were numb and everyone was bundled up. It was challenging just to shoot. My bow was more forgiving to shoot accurately than the speedier setups. I feel this is a good mindset for the average bowhunter. Set up your bow to be forgiving of human errors and the less-than-perfect shooting form frequently found in the odd stances and tough circumstances of hunting.

If you don't make a good shot at a steel silhouette target, the arrow will be destroyed upon impact.

Similarities to Hunting

Many of the components in 3-D shooting are just like those you encounter while hunting.

Stance

As in hunting, you frequently have to shoot 3-D targets from awkward stances. The more variation in body posture you learn to shoot accurately from, the more proficient a hunter you will become. My buddy, Gordon Allington, started out his archery interest as a paper puncher and then caught the 3-D bug. I distinctly recall him telling me after his first 3-D shoot, "I couldn't believe how awkward it was to shoot while kneeling or standing on uneven terrain," he said. "This makes it a lot harder to maintain good form and still shoot accurately. I'm used to standing on a level, cement floor and shooting at 20 yards [18 m]."

Interference

Awkward shooting stances frequently come with interference problems. The two most common are the bowstring with clothing and bow limbs with brush. When possible, I recommend wearing hunting clothes during 3-D shoots. It's a lot less aggravating to miss a target due to the bowstring slapping your hunting coat than missing perhaps the only chance of the year on a nice buck.

Good form, proper draw length and an arm guard should prevent clothes-to-bow-string interference. However, training yourself to check for small limbs that might interfere with bow limbs or wheels upon release is much more difficult—especially when game is present. What generally happens is, your concentration is directed toward the target/animal and shooting a good arrow. Then, your bow limb smacks a branch and sends your arrow awry. Remember, your bow limbs and wheels are moving a considerable distance between the full-draw and relaxed positions. If the natural motion of the top bow limb is obstructed, it will send your arrow high and vice versa for lower-limb interference. A quick check for brush before you draw and then again when anchoring will eliminate this problem in 3-D shooting and hunting.

There is one more interference problem that will drive you crazy in both archery aspects. It's the unseen twig partway to the target. Unless you consciously check for small twigs, you'll look right past them. When time allows, I like to look through binoculars at my arrow's predicted flight path to the quarry before shooting. If you learn to identify these obstacles before releasing, you can frequently shoot around or over them.

On one moose hunt, I drew and let down on six bulls at less than 35 yards (32 m). Each time there was brush obscuring the arrow's flight path. Then, I finally got what I thought was a clear shot on a bruiser bull. It seemed like slow motion as the arrow arched beautifully over the brush only to deflect off one wispy willow branch and bury harmlessly into the powdered snow. With the large kill zone on a moose, it would have been easy to aim an inch or two (few centimeters) on either side of the twig—had I noticed it.

Pressure

Another aspect of 3-D tournaments I find helpful in making me a more successful bowhunter is the peer pressure of trying to make a good shot while all my buddies are breathing down my neck. Although this pressure, or intimidation, is not exactly the same as shooting at game, I think it can build confidence if you have the right attitude.

I'm not very sympathetic of the guy who says, "I shoot a lot better by myself—especially in the backyard when no one is watching." I say if you can't accurately thump a chunk of foam with a handful of people watching, you're not likely to maintain composure while drawing down on a deer either. The more experience you have shooting in stress-

ful situations, whether it's peer pressure or at game, the better off you'll be.

Pick a Spot

One of the most beneficial aspects of 3-D shooting from a bowhunter's mindset is the opportunity to "pick a spot." I strongly believe learning to pick a spot while shooting at game is one of the most difficult things to master. Since 3-D targets are made so realistically now, it's easy to use the contours of the target to help with aiming—just as on an animal.

Recently, I reaffirmed the difficulty of picking a spot.

I was practicing in my backyard, making sure my sights were on and the broadheads flew to the same point of impact as the field tips. Thus, I shot at a 2-inch (5-cm) aiming dot. The broadheads flew beautifully, just like my field tips, and my sights were dead-on. I was shooting softball-size groups or smaller out to 60 yards (55 m).

Then I switched to an animal-face paper target. The first couple groups were terrible. I stopped for

As hunting season approaches, begin shooting at animal-like targets; it forces you to pick a spot.

a moment and scratched my bald head. "What's going on here?" I asked myself. Then it dawned on me, "You're not concentrating on a spot, you're just shooting at the front half of the animal." I settled down and proceeded to shoot much better after that.

While hunting, you may only get a few opportunities per year to pick a spot. But you can practice picking a spot all year long at 3-D shoots.

Range Estimation

The fact the targets are three-dimensional is a benefit for the bowhunter, too. When shooting at a spot target, it's hard to estimate where an arrow would hit an animal. With the 3-D targets, you know right away how good of a shot you made. Also, when shooting at angles other than broadside, you can examine the angle of penetration the arrow would take.

There's one more major similarity between 3-D shooting and bowhunting. Three-D shooting is great practice for range estimation. Your distance-judging skills easily transfer to hunting.

I try to judge right down to the exact yard. Then, I stick with that decision. Even with the faster bows, a 3-yard (2.7-m) error in yardage estimation will cause high or low impacts. Don't second-guess

This shooter is scoring and pulling his arrows from a McKenzie 3-D target.

your estimation; just shoot the best arrow you can. If the arrow hits above or below the kill zone, you shot a good arrow—just misjudged the yardage. If you start second-guessing and pushing or flinching the shot, however, it may cause windage impact problems, too.

I like to shoot high 3-D scores as much as anyone. But, I keep my hunter's perspective. At the end of the day I'll ask myself how many shots were correct for a lethal hit on a real animal.

After a handful of 3-D shoots you'll start to formulate some opinions about range estimation. Here's what I've learned: In flat, open country I have a tendency to think the target is closer. While shooting in heavily forested terrain, I think the opposite. The tunnel effect of looking through a wooded corridor makes the target appear farther away than it really is. Other archers have told me they perceive these situations just the opposite. It's something you have to learn for yourself.

If a target is placed slightly over a rise, partly shielded by a log or across a gully, it's more difficult to judge because you can't see the terrain beyond that obstacle. Another pitfall is using the animal's size to help estimate yardage. This is not reliable. In 3-D shooting there are targets of various sizes—just as nature makes different sizes of deer.

I recall a tournament when shooting with my buddy, Sam Hunt. He was missing high or low more frequently than he would like to admit. I asked how he was judging distance. He replied, "I just look at the size of the animal and shoot." I then asked if he realized there were two different sizes of deer targets and two kinds of pig targets on this course. He hadn't. I also suggested measuring overland in 20-yard (18 m) increments. By the end of the day he was keeping pace with me. Now I have to shoot my very best to beat him!

The other big advantage to practicing on foam targets before hunting is learning the ups and downs of shooting on steep terrain. Your arrow will impact higher on both uphill and downhill shots than it will at the same yardage on level ground. The more you practice on the steep shots, the better you'll understand how much less yardage to hold for on any given angled shot. (See Chapter 18 for more details.)

Differences from Hunting

Some components of 3-D shooting are almost the opposite of what you strive for when hunting.

Rush to Shoot

With 3-D shooting you have considerable time to estimate yardage, calculate angles and so forth. That isn't always the case while hunting. From personal mistakes and observing others, I believe we have a tendency to rush the shot while hunting. We're afraid the animal will walk or run off. It's crucial to take enough time to do things right yet not so much time that you lose the opportunity. Experience and learning animal behavior will help.

Bow Noise

The 3-D shooter doesn't care about a noisy bow. No matter how loud the bow, a foam target isn't going to jump the string. I believe a quiet bow helps in hunter success. For instance, I think a person shooting a high-poundage, light-arrow setup (where more energy and vibration are transferred into noise instead of into the arrow) is more likely to spook game than a quieter bow shooting a slower arrow.

Scoring and Shot Placement

Most of the shoots I've attended had a 12, 10, 8, and 5 scoring system. It breaks down to 12 points for pinpoint kills, 10 points given for the central kill zone, 8 points for the larger kill zone, and 5 points for a non-vital hit. From a hunter's point of view, if your arrow strikes the animal's vitals, the result is a quick, humane death–the most reverent method of dispatch. It doesn't matter if it's an 8 or a 12.

Also, I'm not convinced the kill zones are completely accurate on some targets. I believe the outer kill zone, or 8-ring, is too large, goes too far forward and is too high on the target. Furthermore, it's detrimental from a hunting standpoint to give credit for non-vital hits. More times than I care to remember, I've heard a shooter say, "Oh, well, at least I hit the target and will get 5 points." I feel this is the wrong attitude for bowhunting. Although we are human and bound to make errors, we should strive for personal excellence in each shot we take. I like the concept of negative scoring for non-vital hits on 3-D targets. Perhaps minus 5 points for non-vital hits. I bet the sting of a really low score on a 3-D course from a handful of non-vital hits would make an archer take notice of bad hits.

Angles

Another portion of the current 3-D scoring that differs from hunting has to do with angled shots. In 3-D, you shoot for score, not necessarily where you'd aim on a quartering-away deer while hunting. Depending on the angle of the shot, often, it would be better to aim for the back of the 8 ring or even into the area counted as a 5. Numerous times, from a hunter's view, I've shot for the kill and not the score. On the target the arrow enters as a 5 score. It would actually angle into the vitals more effectively than a hit that enters in the 10-ring. This shot placement may cause the arrow to penetrate in front of a live animal's vitals.

As long as every 3-D target is placed exactly broadside this isn't a problem. However, I've yet to shoot a 3-D tournament with every target precisely broadside. For the experienced hunter this isn't a problem. He or she knows where to hold on angling shots. However, for the newcomer it could have a negative influence.

Conditioning

Finally, I'm frequently winded, exhausted, frozen to the core or shaking while adrenline surges through my veins when I'm about to shoot at game. This is seldom the case while shooting 3-D targets.

Phil Lincoln shows the difference between proper point of aim for a broadside shot (left arrow) and where you should aim for a kill shot when game is quartering away (right arrow).

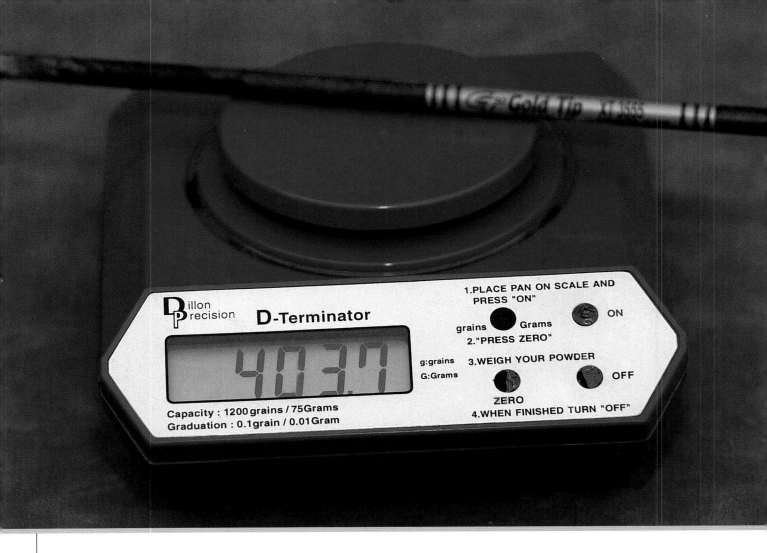

CHAPTER THIRTEEN

Building Arrows

Custom building arrows is a tedious and labor-intensive process, period. Yet, if you have a touch of craftsmanship in your veins, some spare time and the capital to purchase the needed tools, specially constructed arrows can improve accuracy and bolster shooting confidence considerably.

How much better will you shoot with custom-built arrows? That's difficult to quantify. It will depend on how well tuned your equipment is, how consistent your form is and just how far you go with custom building arrows. I know I shoot much more accurately and confidently since I started custom building my arrows. There's really nothing better than knowing your equipment will perform flawlessly.

If you're not the patient type, you are better off buying prefabricated custom arrows, such as True Flight's Pro Series arrows. Another shortcut is to spend more money upfront on those arrows most likely to shoot great right out of the box, such as Easton's ACC aluminum/carbon composites.

If you choose the custom-built-arrow route, the following equipment list and procedure steps should be helpful.

Equipment

Here is a short list of what I consider must-haves if you're going to custom build arrows:

• First, you must have an arrow cut-off saw. I've been using the same Easton model for so long I can't remember what it cost. Nowadays, cut-off saws range in price from about $100 to $250.

• Second, you'll want a spine-deflection tester to maximize results with custom arrows. I use a Carbon QC Arrow Spine Tester made by Ram Products. It costs about $250 but it serves multiple purposes. Besides testing spine deflection, this machine checks arrow straightness to within 0.0005 inch (0.0127 mm). It also checks broadhead and nock run-out for concentricity to within 0.0005 inch.

• You'll also need an accurate grain scale. I have a $300 Dillion Precision electronic grain scale originally designed for weighing ammunition-reloading components. It works great for weighing arrow parts and pieces, too.

• Next is a fletching jig. I've used the same $60 Bitzenburger fletching jig for more than twenty years. It is rugged and simple, and fletches arrows very consistently.

• Another handy tool for custom building arrows is the Arrow Squaring Device made by G5 Outdoors (approximately $30 for aluminum arrows and $36 for carbon arrows).

• Finally, owning or at least having access to a shooting machine is ideal. One of them can run you $1,200.

If the price of equipment for building custom arrows hasn't scared you off, read on.

Procedures

Although building arrows is not all that complicated, here's the sequence I recommend:

Step 1: Sort Raw Shafts

Many small steps are involved in this first big step. Checking shafts for consistent spine deflection, straightness and weight as well as batching nocks and inserts by weight are all part of the sorting

Sam Miller uses an Easton high-speed arrow cut-off saw. G5's Arrow Squaring Device (inset) is a nifty tool to ensure a precise 90-degree end.

process. Additionally, indexing the nocks vertically to the stiff side of each arrow will dramatically improve accuracy.

When starting with 36 shafts, you may end up with several batches of components to keep their spine, straightness and weight within pinpoint shooting tolerances. The number and size of the batches will depend on your shooting skills, preferences, the variances of a given manufacturer's production and what your arrow budget will allow.

I've had excellent results with Gold Tip carbon arrows arriving from the factory with tight tolerances in weight and straightness. Carbon Tech currently has the tightest tolerances in spine deflection among all the carbon arrows on the market.

Step 2: Make a Straight Cut

After sorting and batching raw shafts, cut one end to a perfect 90-degree angle with an arrow cut-off saw. It's worth the extra time during the initial set-up of a new saw to ensure it's going to trim arrows at a true 90-degree angle. If you don't, wobbling broadheads and nocks will occur and consistent flight will be diminished right away.

Another handy device for truing up each end of the arrow is G5's Arrow Squaring Device. I have both models they offer: one for carbon arrows and the other for aluminum. I use the aluminum model to square up insert ends for perfect broadhead concentricity.

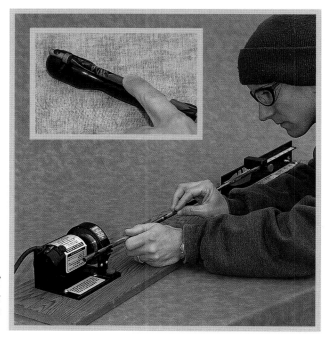

According to Jerry Thompson of Ram Products, the designer of the Carbon QC Spine Tester and a serious bowhunter/tournament archer, "Highly accurate arrows begin with a solid foundation. If you are shooting aluminum arrows, you will find that because of the tried-and-true manufacturing process, they are very consistent within a manufacturing batch, with regard to spine and straightness. This is why most accomplished indoor and field archers rely on aluminum or aluminum/carbon composite shafts for tournament shooting.

"Conversely, carbon arrows vary greatly within a sample group. This is due to the manufacturing process and the inherent material properties. We believe the benefits of carbon arrows (durability, stiffness, light weight, flatter trajectory and cost) make it worthwhile to tune carbon arrows to achieve tournament-level accuracy. Carbon arrows hold their custom tune much better than aluminum arrows.

"We generally use four discrete processes before fletching arrows: sorting arrows by spine, indexing the nocks in relation to the stiffest side of the shaft, checking the straightness from nock to tip and sorting by weight.

"Arrow spine within a dozen carbon arrows can vary by as much as 0.060 inch [1.5 mm], which is equivalent of shooting 11 arrows with 340 spine deflection and one with 400 spine of the same weight," Thompson said. "Some manufacturers are more prone to variation than others. But all brands of arrows can be improved upon by using the Carbon QC Arrow Spine Tester. In addition to arrows varying in spine within a given batch, they also vary in spine around the diameter of each individual shaft. It's not uncommon to find an arrow that, when viewed from the end, will have a 0.340-inch [8.636-mm] spine deflection at 12 o'clock, 0.345 inch [8.763 mm] at 3 o'clock, 0.375 inch [9.525 mm] at 6 o'clock and back to 0.345 inch [8.763 mm] at 9 o'clock.

"Thus, arrow sorting is the process of measuring the spine of a large group of arrows and then placing them into smaller groups with consistent spine. This ensures all arrows within a group are flexing the same amount during the launch cycle. This is particularly important when shooting arrows with fixed-blade broadheads. The exposed blades compete with the fletches for flight control.

"By checking and marking the stiff side of the arrow with a felt-tip pen, then recording all arrow spines, it will become evident some arrows are much stiffer than others. You can start with several dozen arrows and sort them into two or three groups or simply cull out the worst ones. It's not possible to give a hard-and-fast benchmark as to how much deviation is too much.

"I believe indexing nocks vertically to the stiff side of each arrow and then fletching the vanes accordingly is most important. Next is keeping the spine deflection from one shaft to the next within 0.006 inch [0.152 mm] and no more than 0.010 inch [0.254 mm] difference from one side of the arrow to the other. Finally, I like my arrows no more than 0.003 inch [0.076 mm] out from being perfectly straight and their weight to within 2 grains [0.13 g] of each other.

"When I sort my arrows to these standards, I get similar results to shoot-tuning arrows with a shooting machine. Moreover, since I started culling and batching my carbon arrows, I've consistently shot 300s during my NFAA indoor league when shooting with my hunting tackle. Before all this sorting, I'd usually shoot 297 to 299."

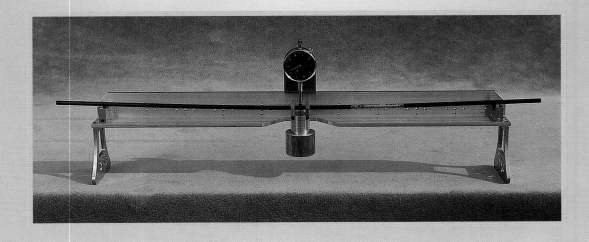

Step 3: Install Nocks

Install nocks to correspond to the felt-pen mark indicating the stiff side of the arrow. Then check for nock-to-arrow concentricity by spinning the arrow and looking for any wobble. Again, personal tolerances may vary but no more than 0.004 inch (0.102 mm) is a good starting point.

Step 4: Fletch Arrows

One of the most direct routes to fletching arrows properly is getting advice from a trusted pro-shop clerk. They fletch hundreds of dozens of arrows every year. Thus, they know which cleaning solvents, fletches and adhesives work best for specific shaft materials and various brands of fletching.

Regardless of chosen components, thorough cleaning of the shaft and fletch base is necessary to ensure secure adhesion. Also, to improve overall accuracy, use a consistent jig so each fletch on every arrow is identical. Be sure to fletch the cock vane in line with the stiff spine mark and indexed nock for super-consistent arrow flight.

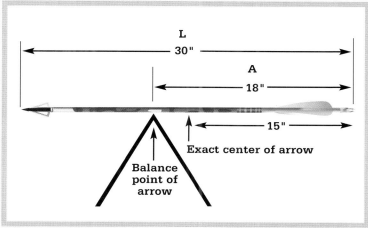

To calculate FOC, use this formula: $[100 (A - \frac{1}{2}L)] \div L$.

In the example above, $100 (18 - 15) \div 30$ equals $100 (3) \div 30$, or $300 \div 30$, or 10% FOC.

At this point I believe it's best to fletch only a few arrows. First, experiment until you get the accuracy results you're looking for. Then, fletch all remaining shafts in a consistent manner.

Step 5: Experiment with Front-of-Center (FOC)

Cut one fletched arrow to the desired length and install an insert without gluing it in place. Thread in your preferred broadhead and check the arrow for its "front-of-center" balance point. For optimum broadhead-tipped arrow flight you'll want at least 8 percent FOC. Achieving between 10 and 15 percent FOC will provide even more stable flight characteristics when shooting with broadheads.

You can increase FOC by decreasing overall fletch and nock weight or by adding more tip weight with a heavier broadhead, heavier insert or with add-on weights screwed into the insert. Also, shortening the arrow length (all else being equal) will increase FOC.

Once you have an arrow, nock, fletch, insert and broadhead combination with about 10 percent FOC, you can complete the arrow-building process and start shooting. You can either take my word that arrows with at least 10 and up to 15 percent FOC will group better with broadheads, or you can make a few arrows with different FOC and shoot-test them yourself.

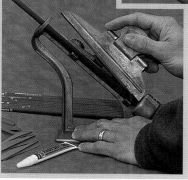

Put a thin bead of glue on the base of a plastic vane in the clamp of the fletching jig (right). Place the clamp onto the fletching jig; leave the vane in the clamp until the glue sets (bottom).

Step 6: Cut Shafts to Length

Once you are satisfied with the FOC of your complete arrows, cut them to length. Next, use a stiff wire brush (like those used for cleaning a rifle barrel) to score the inside wall of the shaft. Then clean it thoroughly with a cotton swab dampened with alcohol or acetone. These small, time-consuming steps will make for a more secure adhesion with the insert. It's frustrating and costly when pulling arrows from a dense target or animal to have the broadhead/insert pull free from the shaft!

Step 7: Install Inserts

Attach broadheads or field tips to inserts. Then wipe the inserts with a clean cloth dampened with alcohol or acetone. Use hot-melt glue for aluminum arrows and two-part epoxy or the adhesive recommended by your pro shop for carbon arrows.

Step 8: Align Broadheads

With aluminum arrows, reheating inserts and rotating the broadhead/insert for consistent fletch-to-broadhead alignment is a snap. With carbon arrows, it's easiest to align the broadheads at the time of gluing in the inserts.

Most experts agree that either lining up the three broadhead blades with the fletches or placing the blades to split the difference between the fletches provide the most aerodynamic arrangements. For two-blade broadheads, it's best to line up the blades horizontally to the bowstring. This will reduce broadhead planing caused by arrow flex upon launch. However you line up the broadhead blades with the fletches, do it consistently for all your arrows. After gluing and aligning, stand the arrows on the broadhead so the weight of the arrow will keep the insert seated until the glue cures.

Be sure to check every broadhead/arrow combination for excellent concentricity. The easiest method is to spin the arrow on the broadhead tip like a top, and look for any wobble. The Carbon

QC Arrow Tester can check broadhead run-out to 0.0005 inch (0.0127 mm) for the most discriminating archers. Most misalignment can be corrected by changing a given broadhead to another arrow, retightening, rotating the insert within the arrow shaft or slightly bending the broadhead ferrule.

Sometimes you'll end up with an arrow, insert and broadhead combination that won't spin true. In this case, it's best to remove the broadhead and only shoot that arrow with a field tip. Whatever you do, don't use a wobbling broadhead/arrow for hunting. It'll surely veer off course and no one knows where it might impact!

Step 9: Group-Tune Arrows

At this juncture, it's wise to either number or name each arrow. Then, in ideal conditions, start shooting arrow groups. Record group size and note any arrows that seem to fly differently than the rest. Of course, the best way to group-tune arrows is with the aid of a shooting machine (see sidebar on page 81).

Step 10: Examine Arrows Before Hunting

Before placing arrows into your quiver and prior to the hunt, do a spot check with each projectile. Check every arrow for straightness by spinning it. Check structural soundness by flexing it. Then, inspect each fletch for good adhesion, and make sure every broadhead blade is secure in the ferrule and each blade is sharp. There's nothing more frustrating than doing everything right as a bowhunter only to have one tiny glitch in your equipment alter shooting results.

Furthermore, I believe shooting "virgin" arrows leaves too much to fate. I prefer to hunt with the arrows I've practiced with. That way I know for sure how each arrow flies. I simply resharpen or install new, sharp broadhead blades. I'm more confident when hunting with those "experienced" arrows that have proven to be accurate.

SHOOTING MACHINE RESULTS

I was fortunate to spend time with the knowledgeable folks at Spot-Hogg Archery Products and their "Hooter Shooter" shooting machine. During our tests, I learned about the individual "personalities" of arrows within a given batch of shafts. We took four Gold Tip arrows with field tips that I'd personally checked for consistent weight and straightness and shot them out of the shooting machine. Indoors, at 20 yards (18 m), each arrow impacted in the exact same hole in the cardboard, shot after shot, without even slightly rounding out the hole! They were perfectly consistent within themselves. However, each of the four arrows impacted to a different spot on the target resulting in an arrow group measuring 1½ inches (3.8 cm) tall by about ½ inch (1.3 cm) wide.

Just by rotating the nocks within the shafts and re-shooting we were able to get three of the four arrows to hit in exactly the same hole. The best we could do (within a reasonable time frame) with the fourth arrow was to adjust the nock orientation until it made the arrow impact to within half of a shaft diameter of the other three. Thus, just by rotating nocks we were able to reduce the arrow group size from 1½ inches (3.8 cm) to ⅜ inch (9.5 mm).

After group-tuning thousands of arrows out of the Hooter Shooter, the folks at Spot-Hogg have determined it's a lack of internal arrow-shaft-to-nock concentricity and variation in spine from one shaft to the next that causes arrows of identical weight and straightness to impact differently.

In general, the Spot-Hogg experts have determined that due to manufacturing methods, aluminum arrows and carbon/aluminum composite shafts are most likely to group-tune best directly out of the box. The wrapped carbon arrows take a little more time to tune but are more likely to maintain their "tune" than aluminum or carbon/aluminum composite shafts when shot repeatedly.

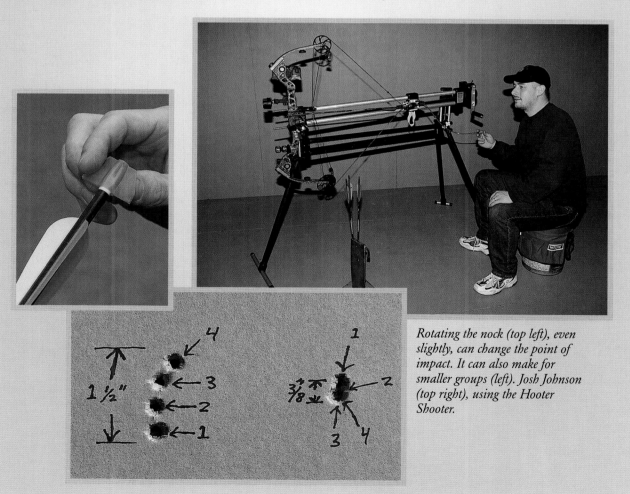

Rotating the nock (top left), even slightly, can change the point of impact. It can also make for smaller groups (left). Josh Johnson (top right), using the Hooter Shooter.

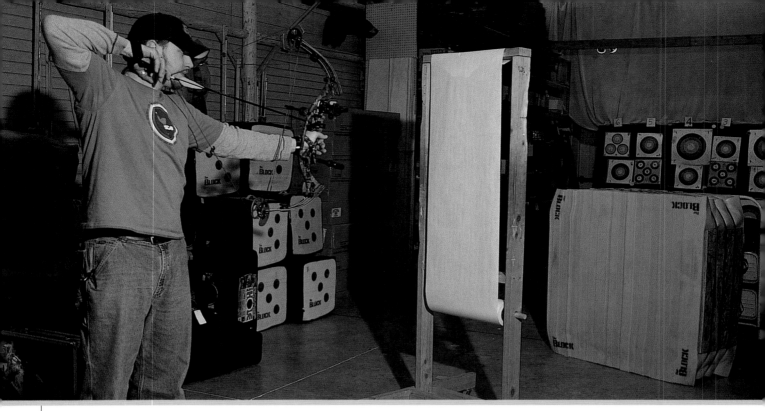

Josh Jones of Spokane Valley Archery paper-tunes an arrow.

CHAPTER FOURTEEN

Bow Tuning

Many bowhunters perceive bow and arrow tuning as magic. Yes, tuning a bow and arrow can be complicated and there is a lot to remember. But if you take your time, set up the equipment properly, select matched components and understand tuning principles, it's less than magical. Bow tuning is usually a straightforward process to produce straightforward results.

The ultimate goal is to achieve an extremely straight arrow launch, shot after shot. A slight wobble in target arrows isn't crucial as long as the point of impact is repeatable. Conversely, broadheads on wobbly arrows can spell disaster for the bowhunter. First, when broadhead blades start competing with fletches for steering control, wind planing and inconsistent point of impact occurs. If you combine inconsistent shooting form with wobbling, broadhead-tipped arrows, accuracy diminishes greatly.

Second, if a broadhead-tipped arrow hits an animal in any manner except point-on, penetration is reduced. For humane reasons, every responsible bowhunter should be deeply concerned about a well-placed arrow with sufficient penetration. The best way to obtain these results is with a well-tuned bow rig.

Learning the perplexities of "arrow dynamics" can be daunting at first. Take your time, learn one tuning method that works for you and stick with it. Who knows? You may even become one of those tuning gurus many bowhunters admire. In the end, grasping the mystical realm of bow/arrow tuning will dramatically improve broadhead-tipped arrow flight and make you a more accurate archer.

Tuning Basics

Some call it bow tuning, others call it arrow tuning. Regardless of title, it's manipulating equipment to achieve optimum results with a given bow, arrow and shooter. The slightest change whatsoever in the equipment or a change in your shooting form could alter bow tune, consequently changing arrow flight and point of impact. Every bow rig, arrow, broadhead and hunter combination creates a unique set of "arrow dynamics."

Just because your buddy's bow is set up a particular way and your bow and draw lengths are similar doesn't necessarily mean you can achieve the same results. I have tried on numerous occasions to set up two bows with identical specifications. I've yet to get them tuned and shooting exactly the same. However, I have been able to get them both to shoot very well.

Clearly, if your shooting form is not consistent, you can't expect tuning results to be consistent. Also, I don't believe in having someone else tune your bow. He or she certainly cannot duplicate your shooting form. Thus, tuning results may vary. Besides, who's going to be shooting your bow come crunch time, you or the person in the pro shop?

However, it doesn't hurt to compare how your bow performs in the hands of an expert or how you stack up against a shooting machine. It stands to reason that if the expert or the machine can make the arrows fly true, with good form, you should be able to do the same. Don't get hung up on these comparisons, though. What really matters is having your bow launching a broadhead-tipped arrow flying true to its mark with you at the helm.

Arrow Spine

To streamline the tuning process, the prepared bowhunter must understand the numerous factors affecting the tune of a rig. The most important aspect is comprehending the two types of arrow spine: static and dynamic.

Static spine is the amount of deflection or bend in the shaft when it's supported at each end and a weight is hung from the center. The more bend, the weaker the spine. Static spine is dictated by shaft diameter, wall thickness and arrow material.

Dynamic spine is apparent only during the launch phase of the shot cycle. Upon release, the bow's energy, through the string, quickly thrusts the arrow forward. This causes column loading and bends the arrow. You'll quickly understand dynamic spine if you get the chance to watch Easton's slow-motion video, "Technical Video Bulletin #1." You can't eliminate this paradox. The trick is to tame it for consistent arrow flight.

Many of the factors affecting dynamic spine include arrow mass weight, arrow static spine, arrow length, broadhead weight, bow draw weight, nock weight, number of strands and material, bowstring weight, bow efficiency, and type of release. Let's examine how these factors alter an arrow's dynamic spine.

• Arrow mass weight is most important. Given two arrows of exactly the same static spine but of different mass weight, the heavier arrow acts weaker; the lighter one, stiffer. This is due to inertia and time. The heavier arrow takes longer to get moving and has more time to absorb the bow's energy. Thus it flexes more. Conversely, the lighter-weight arrow takes off quicker and has less time to absorb the bow's energy. It flexes less.

Arrow length, broadhead weight, bow draw weight, nock weight, number of bowstring strands and the string's mass weight all follow this principle, too. All else being equal, longer arrows (consequently heavier) act weaker. Shorter arrows act stiffer.

• A heavier broadhead will weaken spine. A lighter head makes the same arrow act stiffer.

• Increasing draw weight makes the same arrow act weaker and vice versa.

• Using fewer bowstring strands will slightly weaken arrow spine as will using a lighter string material.

• A bow with a more efficient energy-storing design (hard-cam bow compared to round-wheel bow) shot at the same draw weight will make the same arrow act weaker.

• A bowhunter using a mechanical release aid can more smoothly launch an arrow of weaker spine than a finger shooter can—all else being equal. Also, when shooting with a finger release, all these aspects are considerably more important to the tuning process than when shooting with a release aid. A bow designed with straight and level nock travel and the arrow launched with a release aid allows for much greater latitude on arrow spine and all these other contributing factors.

For example, with my current Mathews bow, I can shoot several arrows of different spine and weight with little or no adjustment to the bow. When I used to shoot with fingers, I had to work much harder to find the right arrow spine, by manipulating the arrow length, point weight, bow draw weight, etc.

I realize this is a lot of technical information to absorb. But once you've tuned a few bow/arrow rigs and have seen the cause and effect of some of these factors, it will start to make sense.

Preparation for Tuning

Most tuning problems can be minimized with proper initial setup. All the following adjustments are approximate settings to get you in the ballpark. Precise adjustment will come when you are paper tuning or bare-shaft tuning the arrow's flight. Whichever method you use, always make one adjustment at a time. Once you've done these preliminary settings a few times, you'll get a sense for what works for you and your equipment. With practice, you can get pretty close by "eyeballing" the settings. On many occasions I've been able to guesstimate my bow/arrow tune settings and then only needed to shoot a few arrows to achieve excellent arrow flight.

Step 1: Install Accessories

Have your bow "hunting ready." If you hunt with a quiver full of arrows and a stabilizer, tune it that way. Don't tune and then add a peep and string silencer or change broadheads or the arrow rest, etc. It could nullify your tuning efforts. Now's the time to set your correct draw length, adjust to a comfortable draw weight and the approximate poundage to coincide with arrow spine. Refer to an arrow-spine chart for reassurance.

Step 2: Set Limb Tiller

Mark your limb bolts with a felt-tip pen to keep track of equal limb tension and poundage. It's really difficult to tune or shoot accurately when the bow limbs and wheels aren't working in unison.

On a two-cam bow, set the limb tiller so top and bottom limbs measure the same distance from back of the limb/riser joint to the string (at 90 degrees to the string). This is accomplished by tightening or loosening one or both limb bolts to get an equal measurement. The purpose of checking the tiller is to ensure both limbs are flexing similarly to obtain a smooth arrow launch. Well-made bows have factory-tested limbs of similar deflection.

To achieve the proper tiller on a one-cam bow, tighten both limb bolts until they bottom out and then back them off with equal rotations to the desired poundage. Or take a length of thread and pull it tight from axle to axle. Then measure from the back of the limb pockets to this thread to check the tiller.

Step 3: Check and Adjust Wheel Timing

Without properly synchronized wheels on two-cam bows, optimum arrow flight is nearly impossible.

Furthermore, a bow with timed wheels will hold steadier during the aiming process. A bow with untimed wheels feels spongy at full draw and you can almost feel the out-of-synch cams fighting each other. A well-timed bow feels more solid at full draw. Be sure to check the wheel timing when static and at full draw. Of the two, it's more important that the wheels are in synch at full draw.

Most single-cam bows have some type of performance marks. With a twist or two of the bus cable and/or string the cam will orientate for optimum performance. Otherwise, there really isn't much to timing a single-cam bow.

Step 4: Check for Wheel Lean

Cam lean definitely has an effect on tunability and forgiving shooting characteristics. By placing a laser tool on one wheel and projecting the beam's dot onto the other wheel, you can visualize just how much the cams are leaning.

Wheel lean is caused by the bus cable being pulled laterally against the cable guard. All bows have some wheel lean. The key is to minimize it.

With a two-cam bow sporting a split-harness cable system, you can adjust wheel lean on both ends.

With a single-cam bow you can only correct the lean of the idler wheel.

To adjust wheel lean, twist up (and thus shorten) only one side of the harness yoke. To ensure the twists don't even themselves out between the two sides of the yoke when shooting, serve about a 3/4-inch (19.1-mm) section of the bus cable directly below the fork in the split harness. For optimum tuning and shootability, try to balance the wheel lean so at rest the cams lean slightly one way and then at full draw the cams lean slightly the other direction. A forgiving bow will have less than 1/2 inch (12.7 mm) of total wheel lean when checked from the static position and then at full draw.

Step 5: Adjust the Arrow Rest

For an initial center-shot position, close one eye and imagine your string as a saw blade cutting the bow's limbs and riser down the middle. You want your arrow to fly through that theoretical center of the bow. This is especially true for the mechanical-release shooter.

Due to string oscillation caused by a finger release, start with your arrow rest just outside of center-shot. A good starting point for the height of the arrow-rest launcher arm is about the height of the threaded hole in the riser (used for attaching the rest to the riser).

Step 6: Set the Nock

With a bow square and nock pliers, initially adjust the string's nock set or D-loop so the arrow-to-string angle is about 3/8 inch (9.5 mm) above 90 degrees. This setting will make your nocked arrow seem to be slightly sloping downhill from nock to tip in the static position. When at full draw and the cam has rolled over, the arrow will be quite level for a more direct launch. The final setting for the nock could be between dead level and slightly

more than 1/2 inch (12.7 mm) high depending on all the variations involved.

After you have the nock set adjusted, you can slide the peep up or down the string so it's comfortable for aiming.

Step 7: Do the "Powder Test"

This is the final step before tuning. Spray the rearward 8 inches (20 cm) of the shaft, fletches and nock with an aerosol foot-powder spray. You may want to spray the riser shelf and arrow rest, too.

Shoot the coated arrow into a firm backstop so the coated end does not penetrate the target. Then, check to see if any part of the arrow or fletch made undue contact with the arrow rest or riser shelf. If so, you must make adjustments to the initial settings to alleviate the contact. Otherwise, what may appear to be a certain arrow flight flaw is actually fletch interference causing the poor flight.

Spraying powder on the arrow helps you see drag marks. Eliminating the fletch-to-rest contact improves arrow flight and accuracy.

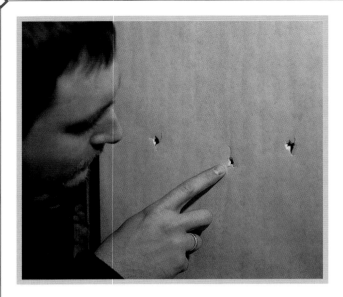

Paper Testing

If you've never paper-tested arrow flight before, it's like reading animal tracks in snow. By understanding those factors that affect dynamic spine covered earlier, you can tell which way an arrow is flying through the paper and what corrections will fix the errant flight.

First obtain some type of framework; a picture frame attached to a tripod will do fine. Next, stretch newspaper or butcher paper over the frame, making sure there is no slack. I prefer butcher paper because the tears read quicker than interpreting an arrow hole through printed newspaper.

If you intend to do a lot of paper tuning, you should consider a more elaborate setup. Years ago my father helped me build a paper-tuning rack made of PVC pipe. It utilizes a large roll of butcher paper and a spring-loaded takeup spool so I don't have to change paper on the frame every five minutes.

Before delving into specific adjustments, here are some basic parameters:

• Shooting through the paper at shoulder height and at right angles ensure the truest reading.

• When paper tuning, the suggested corrections are assuming excellent and repeatable shooting form. If your form is lacking (arrows don't tear consistent-looking holes on every shot) you may want to reread Chapters 7, 8 and 9.

• I recommend shooting through paper at several yardages. It's easy to be fooled by arrow flight after a one-distance paper test. Remember, an arrow virtually explodes out of a bow. Then it stabilizes at the distance it hits the paper but continues wobbling beyond it. I've had arrows shoot near-perfect holes through paper up close but then wobble an inch or two (2.5 to 5 cm) to the right at 6 yards (5.5 m). With proper adjustments I can correct this stiff-acting arrow.

• Start shooting about 6 feet (1.8 m) from the paper when using a release aid, and about 9 feet (2.7 m) away when shooting with fingers. Some folks suggest starting at about 3 feet (1 m) so the fletching doesn't have any time to correct flight flaws. Whichever you choose, remember that your goal is to achieve a straight, clean arrow flight that is represented by a neat hole with three equally balanced tears in the paper where fletches went through, directly behind the arrow point.

• Back up in 3-foot (1-m) increments to about 30 feet (9 m), and shoot several more arrows. This provides an accurate illustration of how the arrow is flying from point-blank to 10 yards (9 m).

• Once you have several identical tears, adjustments can be made. It's important to be patient; make changes one step at a time. Don't be disappointed if perfect arrow flight seems elusive. Upon close inspection, you can tell where the field tip or broadhead broke the paper and where the fletches tore through. This indicates what direction the arrow is wobbling and what changes should improve arrow flight.

All adjustments listed in this chapter are for the right-handed shooter. The corrections are exactly opposite for left-handed shooters. Also, the proper correction can differ if you shoot with fingers or a release, and depending on how cleanly your bow launches arrows (by design). Thus, if you don't get the desired results try the opposite adjustment of what is recommended. Sometimes it works!

Finally, take your time in the tuning process. It's not usually a whiz-bang five-minute deal.

The following examples and correction information should be helpful in paper testing your setup.

PAPER TESTING

This tear indicates good arrow flight. The fletching entered the paper directly behind the point.

This tear indicates a low nocking point. To correct, raise the nocking point 1/16 inch (1.6 mm) at a time and repeat the procedure until the low vertical tear is eliminated.

This tear indicates a high nocking point, clearance problem or a very weak arrow if you are using a release aid. To correct, lower the nocking point 1/16 inch (1.6 mm) at a time until the high tear is eliminated. If, after moving the nocking point a few times, the problem is unchanged, the disturbance is most likely caused by a lack of clearance or by an arrow that is too weak (if using a release aid). To identify a clearance problem, use a powder test to check to see if the arrow fletching is hitting the arrow rest.

Compound with Release (CR)

If no clearance problem exists and you are using a mechanical release, to correct:

1. Try a more flexible arrow rest blade if using a launcher-type rest or reduce downward spring tension on adjustable-tension launcher rests.
2. Decrease peak bow weight if there is an indication the arrow spine is too weak.
3. Reduce the amount the shaft overhangs the contact point on the arrow rest.
4. Choose a stiffer arrow shaft.

This tear indicates a stiff arrow reaction for right-handed archers using finger release (RF, CF). This is an uncommon tear for right-handed compound archers using a mechanical release (CR). However, it can occur and generally indicates that the arrow-rest position is too far to the right or that there is possible vane contact on the inside of the launcher rest.

Finger Release (RF, CF)

To correct:

1. Increase bow weight/peak bow weight.
2. Use a heavier arrow point and/or insert combination.
3. Use a lighter bowstring (fewer strands or lighter material).
4. Use a weaker-spine arrow.
5. Decrease cushion-plunger tension or use a weaker spring on "shoot around" rests.
6. CF only—Move the arrow rest slightly in, toward the bow.

Mechanical Release Aid (CR)

To correct:

1. Move the arrow rest to the left. Continue moving the rest to the left in small increments until the right tear is eliminated.
2. Make sure the arrow has adequate clearance past the cable guard and cables.
3. Make sure the bow hand is well relaxed to eliminate excessive bow-hand torque.

These abbreviations have been used throughout:

RF = Recurve with finger release

CF = Compound with finger release

CR = Compound with release aid

PAPER TESTING CONTINUED

This tear indicates a weak arrow reaction or clearance problem for right-handed finger-release (RF, CF) archers. For right-handed compound shooters using a mechanical release (CR), the left tear is common and usually indicates a weak arrow reaction and/or clearance problem. If a high-left tear exists (see below), make sure you correct the nocking point first before proceeding further.

Finger Release (RF, CF)

To correct:

1. Decrease bow weight/peak bow weight.
2. Use a lighter arrow point and/or insert combination.
3. Use a heavier bowstring (more strands or heavier material).
4. Use a stiffer-spine arrow.
5. Increase cushion-plunger tension or use a stiffer spring on "shoot around" rests.
6. CF only—Move the arrow rest slightly out, away from the bow.

Mechanical Release Aid (CR)

To correct:

1. Move the arrow rest to the right. Continue to move the rest to the right in small increments until the left tear is eliminated.
2. Make sure the bow hand is well relaxed to eliminate excessive bow-hand torque.
3. Decrease peak bow weight.
4. Choose a stiffer-spine arrow.

This tear shows a combnation of more than one flight disturbance. Use the procedures that apply to the tear pattern for your style of shooting, and combine the recommendations, correcting the vertical pattern (nocking point) first, then the horizontal. If you experience a tuning problem (especially with the nocking point location) and are unable to correct a high/low tear in the paper, have your local pro shop, check the "timing" (roll-over) of your eccentric wheels or cams.

These abbreviations have been used throughout:

RF = Recurve with finger release

CF = Compound with finger release

CR = Compound with release aid

Note: Do not combine paper testing and bare-shaft tuning. Alterations for paper testing are based on the nock end of the arrow. Bare-shaft tuning adjustments are based on the point end of the arrow.

Bare-Shaft Tuning and Line Shooting

If you're not set up to paper-tune your arrows, another excellent way to optimize arrow flight is called bare-shaft tuning and line shooting. Learning these methods may be a little easier than paper tuning. Additionally, bare-shaft tuning and line shooting can be accomplished in field conditions should an emergency bow repair (that changes the tune) become necessary.

There are many versions of bare-shaft tuning and line shooting. Below is a modified version I learned from Easton's *Arrow Tuning Guide* and my friend Jim Cowgill. Jim is a dedicated bowhunter and accomplished tournament archer. I've paper-tuned my bow rigs first, and then double-checked the tune via bare-shaft tuning and vice versa. Either way, I get similar results—terrific arrow flight. Proper initial bow setup, such as center-shot, arrow-rest height, nocking-point height, etc., is needed regardless of tuning method.

You can use the following steps for the bare-shaft tuning and line-shooting process.

Step 1: Time the Wheels

Check for smooth wheel rotation and make sure there is little or no lateral play in the wheels.

Step 2: Level the Bow Sight

This will ensure it is plumb with the bowstring. See Chapter 10 for directions.

Step 3: Paper-Tune for a Clean Hole

Do this at about 4 feet (1.2 m) from the paper. This step is just a precaution to make sure the bow/arrow is not so far out of tune that a bare shaft would impact the target sideways and break the arrow. Also, this step may not be feasible in field conditions.

Step 4: Correct Vertical Impact

Shave fletches off one of your hunting arrows until the shaft is clean and free of any fletch remnants or glue. When finished, you'll have a bare shaft with the point and nock in place. If your shooting form is very repeatable, you'll only need one bare shaft. If you are not certain of your form, it may be wise to shoot a couple bare shafts before making adjustments.

For excellent results in bare-shaft tuning, shoot at 16 yards (14.5 m) from the target backstop. The goal is to shoot a group of three normally fletched arrows and one or two bare shafts. You will be comparing the bare shaft's point of impact to the group of fletched arrows.

Optimally, you want the bare shaft to impact within 1 inch (2.5 cm) of the fletched arrows when shot at 16 yards. If necessary, the first adjustment should correct the vertical gap between the bare shaft and the fletched arrows. If the bare shaft impacts above the identically aimed fletched arrows, move the nocking point up on the bow string in 1/16-inch (1.6-mm) increments until the bare shaft and fletched arrows impact at the same elevation. Bare shafts that impact above identically aimed fletched arrows indicate a low nocking point. If the nocking point is too low, it may force the arrow fletching down into the arrow rest, creating clearance problems.

Should the bare shaft impact below the identically aimed fletched arrows, move the nocking point down on the string in 1/16-inch (1.6-mm) increments until the bare shaft impacts at the same elevation or slightly lower than the fletched shaft. It is sometimes desirable to have the bare shaft impact just slightly below the identically aimed fletched shafts.

To ensure you have the correct nocking-point height, repeat the test until the bare shaft groups very close (vertically) to the fletched arrows. For those shooting with a release aid and a string D-loop, it's much easier to move the arrow-rest launcher arm up or down instead of having to move the D-loop.

Step 5: Correct Horizontal Impact

Now that you have the bare shaft impacting close to the fletched arrows in a vertical manner, you want to close the horizontal gap next. If the bare shaft impacts left of the identically aimed fletched arrows, that means the arrows are acting too stiff in spine. To correct this, increase bow draw weight, increase arrow point weight, shoot a longer arrow or move the arrow rest away from the riser.

If the bare shaft impacts to the right of the identically aimed fletched arrows, that means the arrows are acting too weak in spine. To correct this, decrease bow draw weight, decrease arrow point weight, shoot a shorter arrow or move the arrow rest closer to the riser.

Remember, all the other aspects that affect arrow spine can be used to correct the horizontal disparity between the bare shaft and fletched arrows, too. If you cannot get the bare shaft to shoot within a couple inches (few centimeters) horizontally of the fletched arrows, you may have to switch to different-spined arrows.

Step 6: Make an Aiming-Line Target

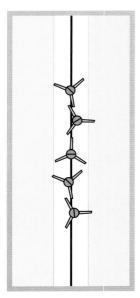

Use cardboard, masking tape and a black felt-tip marker. Run some 1½-inch-wide (38-mm) tape vertically down the center of a 2-foot-tall (60-cm) piece of cardboard. Then draw a vertical ½-inch-wide (12-mm) line down the center of the tape. The aiming-line target should be hung plumb on the backstop.

Next, shoot with fletched arrows (you're done with the bare shaft) at the black centerline from about 4 feet (1.2 m) away. Adjust the bow sight until you are hitting dead-on vertically. Make sure you aim a little higher and lower along the black line with each arrow so as not to damage any nocks or shafts.

Then, move your aiming-line target out to 40 yards (36 m). Aiming at the vertical black line at the farther distance, shoot several arrows.

If necessary, move the arrow rest in or out slightly until the arrows impact very close to the centerline. Double-check at the 4-foot (1.2-m) distance to ensure the arrows are still hitting vertically along the centerline. At this point, don't move the sight; move only the arrow rest until the arrows impact along the centerline at both distances.

At this point your bow/arrow/shooter combination is tuned better than most. The bare shaft helped adjust the nock position and the aiming-line test helped with arrow spine and center-shot.

Step 7: Horizontal Fine-Tuning

Turn the aiming-line target horizontally. Make sure it is level. Shoot several arrows with your best form at the aiming-line target from 60 yards (55 m) away.

You are checking for high and low groups along the centerline. Either move the nock set up or down, or the arrow-rest launcher arm up or down in minute increments to obtain the tightest group possible (horizontally along the centerline).

This step alone could take several arrow groups over several days, depending on your shooting fitness and how consistently you can shoot.

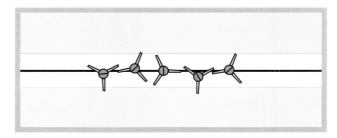

Step 8: Vertical Fine-Tuning

At 60 yards (55 m), hang the aiming-line target vertical and plumb. Shoot your best groups along the centerline. With minute adjustments (1/64 inch/0.4 mm) move the arrow rest in or out to obtain the tightest vertical groups possible. In time, you'll have a bow rig that'll launch arrows capable of incredibly accurate results.

Broadhead Tuning

In general terms, broadhead tuning is done by first shooting a group of arrows with field points into the target, and then by shooting a group of arrows with broadheads. The two groups are compared and the appropriate adjustments are made.

CAUTION: Never shoot unfletched or bare shafts with broadheads—flight is extremely erratic and dangerous!

The field points should be as close in weight and length as possible to the weight and length of the broadheads. Because it is necessary to first establish a good group with field points, broadhead tuning can be done only after acceptable tuning has been established with field points (see Paper Testing or Bare-Shaft Tuning earlier in this chapter).

Shoot a Group with Field Points

Set up a suitable broadhead target at a distance of 20 to 30 yards (18 to 27 m) or farther if your shooting form allows. Using a set of field-tipped arrows that have been tuned with your bow, shoot a group of 3 or 4 arrows into the target. Take care to shoot as tight a group as you are capable.

Shoot a Group with Broadheads

Using the same arrows, tipped with broadheads, shoot a group of 3 or 4 arrows into the target. Use the same aiming spot that was used for the field points. The shot group is the key. If you are content you have shot a respectable group based on your ability, then compare the position of the two groups.

Make the adjustments listed below to your setup and shoot both groups again. Keep adjusting and shooting until both sets (field points and broadheads) group in the same area. The adjustments for broadhead tuning are virtually the same as for bare-shaft tuning.

Make Adjustments

Adjustments sometimes affect more than is expected. It is best to always make the up/down adjustments first. Once the two groups are on the same horizontal plane, then make the left/right adjustments. Here are some guidelines:

• If the broadheads group above the field points (see A below), move the nocking point up.

• If the broadheads group below the field points (see B below), move the nocking point down.

• If the broadheads group to the left (see C below), they are behaving as if the shaft is too stiff (for a right-handed archer). Any, or several, of the following can be done to correct the point of impact:

– Increase the poundage on the bow.

– Change to heavier broadheads.

– If you are using a cushion plunger, decrease the spring tension.

– Move the arrow rest or cushion plunger toward the bow. Make adjustments of $1/32$ inch (0.8 mm) at a time.

• If the broadheads group to the right (see D below), they are behaving as if the shaft is too weak. Any, or several, of the following can be done to correct the point of impact:

– Decrease the poundage on the bow.

– Change to lighter broadheads.

– If you are using a cushion plunger, increase the spring tension.

– Move the arrow rest or cushion plunger away from the bow. Make changes $1/32$ inch at a time.

Remember, broadhead tuning can only be accomplished after the bow has been properly set up and tuned with field or target points. If these adjustments don't encourage broadhead-tipped and field-tipped arrow groups to converge, you may need to shoot a longer (thus weaker-acting) arrow or shorter (thus stiffer) arrow. Changing to a different spined arrow may be in order, too.

Finally, there are many bow/arrow/broadhead/archer combinations where broadheads and field tips just won't hit the same point of impact—due to aerodynamic differences. If this is the case, as long as the broadhead-tipped arrows group well, merely sight in and practice with broadheads. From a bowhunter's perspective, it doesn't matter where your field tips impact a target. It does matter where your broadhead hits an animal!

Field Point Group   *Broadhead Group*

Lon with a 69-inch bull moose taken at 30 yards with one well-placed arrow.

CHAPTER FIFTEEN

Effective Shooting Range

One question is as old as bowhunting itself: How far is too far when shooting at big game with a bow and arrow? There is no easy answer, and that just adds to the overall challenge of bowhunting. You must recognize that every bowhunting shot opportunity is a unique set of variables; just as you are a unique individual with shooting skills and a mental composure that may change from one shot to the next. Plus, there are tons of aspects to consider. To complicate matters, most of the time, those decisions must be made in a fleeting moment.

Here are some guidelines to help determine your effective shooting range.

Know Your Limits

If there ever were a time to be completely honest with yourself, it's when choosing to shoot an arrow at game. You must know your personal limits and only shoot when certain you can make the shot. Loosing an arrow when the situation is "iffy" is not ethical. Throughout this book I've stated I do miss and I have made bad hits. That's part of bowhunting. But, I never shoot an arrow at game without the intent of killing it swiftly with one well-placed arrow. You should do the same.

Shooting skill is a definite consideration. Just because you can hit an apple at 50 yards (45.5 m) doesn't necessarily mean you can ethically shoot a deer at that distance. For example, I know people who can hit a quarter-size bull's-eye at 20 yards (18 m), 60 shots in a row (when shooting an NFAA 300 round) but have trouble hitting a deer at 20 yards. What's the difference? One, the target doesn't move. Two, they get so excited about shooting a deer they fall apart mentally.

We all have different levels of shooting skill and some folks maintain mental composure better than others. There is no concrete rule here but you can use your own shooting experiences as a gauge. Let's say at 20 yards you can shoot four-arrow groups the size of a tennis ball when practicing alone in the backyard. Yet, when at the range with buddies leering over your shoulder, that four-arrow group becomes more the size of a softball. Whether you realize it or not, you are intimidated and self-conscious when others watch you shoot.

Let's take it one step further. In solitary practice, you always keep your arrows within the 10-ring on a 3-D target out to 40 yards (36 m). But when competing in a tournament, you're lucky to hit the 8-ring consistently.

This pattern of enlarging groups under pressure situations must be considered when shooting at game. If you can't maintain composure from peer pressure or tournament pressure, you are not likely to keep it together when shooting at game either. This means your "effective" shooting distance when hunting should be reduced considerably compared to practice situations.

With my abilities, I estimate that I only shoot about half as well in a hunting situation as I do in practice. That means if I shoot 2-inch (5-cm) groups at 30 yards (27 m) on the range, I might be able to hit within a 4-inch (10-cm) circle when hunting—in perfect conditions. Your guidelines should match your abilities.

You can also use 3-D tournament scores as a rough guide. But you must be realistic when comparing foam targets to living creatures. Here's what I do: At the end of each tournament, I take a hard look at my scorecard and every shot scenario. By analyzing whether each shot would have made a humane harvest on game, I come up with a rough

effective range. The parameters I've chosen are: I must average at least an eight-score or a kill on every target out to 60 yards (55 m). To me that means if the animal and the wind are graveyard still and I'm dead calm and everything is perfect, I might take the shot while hunting.

I say "might" take the shot because I must also consider confidence, concentration, my physical state and so on. There have been times in my bowhunting career when I was so confident, that if an animal presented a shot and I chose to shoot, it was a done deal—period! Also, there have been phases when my shooting confidence was in the toilet.

Just a few years ago, when hunting Sitka blacktails on Kodiak Island, I was not shooting very well. I just wasn't consistent. Then, when I lost my laser range finder on the first evening, my effective shooting range shrank to point-blank shots only!

So I relied on what I was most confident about at the time: my hunting abilities. In three days of hunting, I killed two Pope and Young–class bucks.

I stalked the first one to within 13 yards (12 m) and I shot the second one at 9 yards (8 m) after a very challenging five-hour stalk. The way I was shooting, I would not have taken a shot farther than 20 yards (18 m).

Conversely, on a Wyoming mule deer hunt, I could hit a paper plate every single shot at 80 yards

Here's Lon with his 9-yard Alaska Sitka buck.

(73 m). With the aid of a laser range finder I killed a buck at 81 yards (74 m). That's the farthest shot I've ever taken and probably always will be. The buck had his face buried in fresh, green alfalfa with nary a concern, there was no breeze and I knew the exact yardage. I was quite calm and made the shot.

As you can see, there are times when shooting abilities and confidence vary. It's up to you to make the right choice.

Know the Distance

Besides a lack of shooting ability and confidence, the most common reason a bowhunter will miss or make a bad hit is not knowing the yardage to the target animal. Military tests have proven most people are not very good at judging yardage beyond 40 yards (36 m). So, don't expect to be super human when it comes to "guessing" the distance to your quarry. However, with enough stump-shooting and 3-D practice, you'll get a sense regarding just how well you judge yardage.

The more precisely you know the distance, as with the aid of a laser range finder or a deer that's standing in a pre-determined shooting lane, the more confident you'll be. If you purely have to guess the distance, your effective range should be reduced to well within the span you can accurately estimate yardage. Furthermore, this guessing distance will be somewhat altered by the trajectory of your arrow. A person who shoots an extremely flat flying arrow—accurately—could conceivably shoot a bit farther than one whose arrow is more arching.

Know Your Quarry

Often, the quarry itself determines the distance you can effectively shoot. For example, it's logical that your effective shooting distance is much farther when hunting moose than turkey. A gobbler has a kill zone about the size of a man's fist. A bull moose presents a kill zone about the size of a beach ball!

Also, your effective shooting range will be altered depending on how skittish the species is—and, more importantly—how nervous the individual specimen in front of you is at the time. For example, Coues deer, whitetails, pronghorns and turkeys generally are very nervous and skittish creatures. Any given individual among these species can be extremely wary. Conversely, moose, mountain goats, bears and caribou are less "edgy" game. Mountain goats, in particular, are slow to respond. I've killed three billies that just stood there and watched me draw the bow and shoot. On the other hand, I wouldn't think about drawing my bow on a Coues buck when it was looking my way.

It's your responsibility to know the habits of your quarry and anticipate how they will behave in various hunting scenarios.

Recognize Optimum Shot Opportunities

Each time a bow shot at game presents itself, you must determine if it's an optimum or marginal opportunity. Furthermore, you must determine if the situation is going to improve or fall apart. Should you shoot now or wait? In the heat of the moment, you must be decisive and confident. Anything less will lessen your poise and ultimately affect the outcome. This is the time to factor in your shooting skills, confidence, ability to judge yardage, the target animal's disposition and body angle.

You must also consider current weather, lighting and terrain conditions. For example, in waning light, your effective range diminishes with every passing minute. In marginal light you are not likely to see those pesky, arrow-altering twigs you would normally avoid in brighter light. And, it's much harder to pick a spot in low light. Gusting wind, downpouring rain, heavy snow, thick fog and every other form of weather will affect how far is too far.

Additionally, if you are not well versed with your arrow's trajectory and how to shoot in odd positions at steep angles, you must reduce your effective range accordingly.

Avoid Temptation

I've heard bowhunters say silly things like, "My effective shooting range is directly proportional to the size of the buck's antlers!" Or, "I spent $4,000 on this hunt so I've got to kill something—no matter what." It's easy to get caught up in ego, glory, fame, etc. It really doesn't matter how many vacation days you've used, how many blisters or burned calories it took or how expensive and hard-to-draw that tag was. You must be disciplined in shot selection, be true to yourself, and be respectful of your quarry. Following is a prime example.

On a brisk September day I was hunting elk in the Big Belt Range with Central Montana Outfitters. My guide, Jim Kirkpatrick, and I had hunted hard for a week. We'd had a couple close calls but no shot opportunities. At daybreak on the last day, we glassed up a monster bull skylined more than a mile (1.6 km) away and perhaps 1,500 feet (457 m) in elevation above us.

We took off at a blistering pace. It was all I could do to stay within sight of Jim and his long-legged, mountain-conditioned form. About 90 minutes later, I was drenched in sweat, feet burning and flat worn-out from the entire week. Jim was hardly flushed.

When we peaked over a ridge and saw the largest bull elk either one of us had ever seen, it was breathtaking. I slithered out of my daypack, nocked an arrow and searched for a stable rock to stand on. There were six other elk closer than the big bull and countless more milling about on the brushy mountainside. I ranged down the hill. The herd bull was 63 yards (57 m) away and feeding, unaware of our presence. When he walked into a small clearing, I drew my bow and anchored.

Unfortunately, the bull turned, faced my direction and began feeding again. No shot there. I let down and waited. Soon he turned broadside, resumed feeding his way back into the brush and paused. I

started to draw again but a pine bough was hanging directly in front of the bull's vitals.

"Shoot!" Jim whispered urgently.

"I can't," I countered. "There's brush in the way."

"Your arrow will arch over it; shoot," he urged. Jim was looking through binoculars from a different angle and was absolutely correct in his advice. But from my perspective, it looked chancy. I didn't want to just hit that bull; I wanted to kill him swiftly with one well-placed arrow.

The distance wasn't a concern for me. In camp the day before, I had been stacking arrows into golf-ball-size groups at 40 (36 m) yards. And I'd shot several judo-tipped arrows when walking logging roads. The farthest I'd missed any shot out to 60 yards (55 m) was by no more than a couple inches (few centimeters). But I'd botched a shot on a dandy mule deer buck a few days earlier. That event was eating at my confidence. That moment of hesitation cost me the bull of a lifetime.

Shortly, the wind swirled and one of the cows close by caught a whiff of human odor. Like a rodeo ruckus, the entire herd stampeded over the mountain and out of my life forever. I slumped to the ground like a stunned boxer.

Between my fluctuating confidence and the marginal shot opportunity, however, I chose not to shoot. Does it chap me that I didn't trust my experienced guide? Absolutely. But I was the one behind the bow. It was my responsibility to interpret the scenario and decide how far was too far. It still stings that I didn't tag that beautiful bull but I sleep well every night knowing I made the right decision at the given moment.

CHAPTER SIXTEEN

Balancing Accuracy and Arrow Speed

Due to the inherent arching flight path of even the fastest hunting arrow, bowhunters are constantly experimenting with ways to flatten arrow trajectory. To an extent, an arrow with a flatter trajectory can negate yardage estimation errors. As a direct by-product of poor distance judging, archery manufacturers get caught up in what I call the speed craze. They diligently create bows that launch arrows faster and faster.

Unfortunately, many of the features of a fast bow are the same traits that make a bow more difficult to shoot accurately in hunting situations. Archery hunters would be better served if bow makers concentrated more on incorporating features to bolster accuracy and shooter forgiveness. A fast miss is not nearly as impressive as a slow arrow that hits its mark!

Regardless of how manufacturers produce bows, it's your ethical duty to shoot a bow and arrow combination that you can shoot accurately. Don't get me wrong. I think a fast arrow is great, but only if it can be shot with consistent, pinpoint results. It will take some experimenting to come up with the fastest, most stable arrow you can control in hunting situations. Furthermore, there are trade-offs with every alteration you make to your bowhunting setup.

You may be able to manipulate your rig to shoot an arrow 20 fps (6 mps) faster. But it's a bad trade-off if the extra speed widens your broadhead-tipped arrow groups when shooting from an awkward stance by more than what it flattens trajectory. Additionally, you may be able to increase arrow speed and still maintain pinpoint shot placement. But if the extra speed makes the rig too noisy for hunting, that's not good either. Here's an example:

One wet, windy morning while still-hunting for mule deer in Colorado's high country, my buddy, South Cox, and I bumped into a really nice four-point buck.

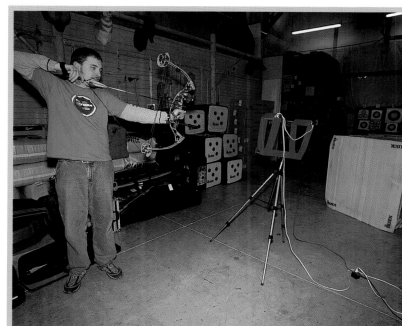

Josh Jones shoots an arrow through a chronograph to check arrow velocity.

The fuzzy-antlered deer was feeding on acorns the rain and wind had knocked off the brush. His head was down and his mouth vacuumed up the protein-rich nuts like a Hoover. The buck was totally unaware of our presence only 37 yards (33.6 m) away.

I'd killed a good buck a couple days earlier in the hunt so it was up to South. Now I've hunted with this self-taught bowhunter for more than a decade and can honestly say he is one of the best clutch shooters in hunting situations I've seen. A 37-yard shot for South is like a slam-dunk for the NBA's Shaquille O'Neal.

I watched through my Swarovski binocular, fully expecting to see South's arrow flick through the buck's chest with pinpoint accuracy. Instead, as if the arrow were flying in slow motion, the buck dropped and spun out of the way before the arrow arrived. The carbon projectile "twanged" into an oak tree like a scene from a cartoon! The buck had jumped the string or, more correctly worded, ducked the arrow. We measured the arrow's height at which it stuck in the tree. Had the deer stayed still, it would have been a lethal shot.

Unfortunately, the sound of the bow going off reached the deer almost four times faster than the arrow. South was shooting a short-brace-height, high-poundage bow with a light carbon arrow. His arrow launched out of the bow at a noisy 290 fps (88.4 mps). But the balance between arrow speed and bow noise was tipped in the buck's favor. I truly believe if South had been shooting my slower arrow out of my quieter bow, that buck would not have reacted so abruptly.

Thus, bow vibration that results in a disturbing and sometimes game-spooking noise must be factored in when balancing arrow speed with accuracy. I must qualify this anecdote with the fact that on the following day, South killed a different buck at a similar yardage with the same noisy bow. For some reason, the second buck didn't react to the sound of the bow as the previous buck had.

Trajectory

Regardless of arrow speed or bow noise, shot placement is priority one for all bowhunters. Additionally, with the advent of laser range finders,

the need for a faster and flatter arrow trajectory is less important now than just a few years ago when we all were "guessing" the yardage to our quarry. I know you can't employ a range finder in every bowhunting shot opportunity. But if you can't confidently estimate the yardage without a laser range finder, then it's probably too far to shoot, regardless of arrow speed!

Although a faster arrow will reach the target animal in a shorter duration and, thus, reduce the chance of the animal moving before the arrow arrives, a fast arrow is not always the best choice for hunting. There are some occasions when a slower arrow will arch over brush and drop into the vitals of the target animal where a faster, flatter flying arrow would deflect off the brush.

One time, I called in a bull moose for a novice bowhunter who was shooting a relatively slow, arching arrow. When the bull stopped at 35 yards (32 m), behind brush, the new bowhunter thought it was a no-shoot situation. Luckily, I had helped him tune, sight in and calculate arrow speed and kinetic energy of his setup. I knew the arrow would lob over the brush and encouraged him to aim right at the moose as if the brush wasn't there. He did and the moose was killed swiftly.

On the other hand, a flatter-flying arrow may be more advantageous when shooting through holes in the brush. My best mule deer to date was killed by shooting straight down through a tennis-ball-size hole in brush. Regardless of arrow speed, it's crucial that you know the arch of your arrow at varying distances. The best way to learn this is through hunting-like practice scenarios.

Kinetic Energy

When determining the fastest arrow you can shoot accurately, remember that downrange trajectory and kinetic energy are two crucial factors to consider. It's easy to make a lighter arrow leave the bow at a faster velocity than a heavier arrow. Using a chronograph, kinetic energy chart and arrow trajectory charts will help. But, the best way is to shoot arrows of different configurations at long range and record the results. Here are some questions you must answer in the process of balancing arrow speed with accuracy.

• How will that light, fast arrow hold up at longer yardages?

• Will the lighter arrow actually impact lower at 60 yards (55 m) than a heavier arrow, due to a greater loss in momentum?

• Will the lighter arrows group as well as the heavier arrows at 60 yards?

• Will that lighter arrow retain enough kinetic energy to provide sufficient penetration at longer distances?

Optimum Setup

Over the years, I've fiddled with various draw-weight bows with different brace heights and cam designs. I've also used a potpourri of arrow and point weights to change the front-of-center, different fletching size and helical, all sorts of broadheads and several arrow materials of varying length. It always seems I come back to about the same setup for consistent accuracy.

The author proudly displays his late-season Colorado mule deer taken with a light, fast carbon arrow.

For my archery abilities, I get good results shooting a bow with 65 to 70 pounds (29.25 to 31.5 kg) of draw weight, about 7½ inches (19 cm) of brace height and a moderate energy cam. For arrows, I like a 27-inch (68.6-cm) shaft weighing about 400 grains (25.92 g) and sporting 4-inch (10-cm) helical vanes on a carbon arrow tipped with a 100- or 125-grain (6.5- or 8-g) broadhead that creates about 10 percent front-of-center. With my short draw length, this type of setup produces arrow speed in the 240- to 250-fps (73- to 76-mps) range and creates about 50 to 55 foot-pounds (6.92 to 7.61 kg-m) of kinetic energy.

Your optimum setup may vary greatly from mine. With considerable experimentation and diligent practice you will reach a point of diminishing return—the extra speed will reduce accuracy to an unacceptable degree. At that point you back off to determine the perfect balance between arrow speed and accuracy.

Ways to Increase Arrow Speed

Many factors affect a bow's ability to launch an arrow at a higher velocity, which in turn flattens arrow trajectory. Flatter trajectory is a good thing because it increases the margin for human error in range estimation. Below is a list of some common ways to increase arrow speed, and the potential trade-offs if you overdo it.

Most of these factors make a bow/arrow combination more critical to shoot accurately. Also, when pushing the limits of increased arrow speed, the projectile will be less stable in flight. And, personal injury and equipment damage may occur. Most bow companies recommend shooting at least 5 grains (0.32 g) of arrow weight per pound (0.45 kg) of draw weight. It's up to you to determine the best balance between speed and accuracy based on your shooting and hunting skills.

• Increasing draw weight will improve arrow velocity by about 2 to 3 fps/0.6 to 0.9 mps (depending on the bow's efficiency) for each additional pound (0.45 kg) of draw weight. Too much draw weight is difficult to pull in a smooth, undetected manner when hunting. It's harder to relax and aim steady. All else being equal, a bow with more draw weight will be noisier to shoot.

• Increasing draw length will improve arrow velocity by 7 to 10 fps/2 to 3 mps (depending on the bow's efficiency) for every inch (2.5 cm) of increased draw length. Using a release aid with less distance between the jaw and trigger can increase your effective draw length without altering form. Shooting without a string loop and then increasing draw length by ½ inch (12.7 mm) may increase arrow speed a few fps (mps). Over-extending form or not using a string loop will decrease accuracy to some extent.

• Decreasing arrow weight will improve arrow velocity by about 5 fps (1.5 mps) for each 25-grain (1.62-g) reduction in arrow weight. You can do this by switching to a lighter arrow material, thinner-walled arrow, smaller-diameter arrow or using a lighter insert or broadhead. All else being equal, a lighter arrow will penetrate a few percentage points less than a heavier arrow. Too light of an arrow may not be quite as stable of a projectile and will make the bow noisier upon launch.

• Decreasing fletching size, profile and texture will improve velocity and reduce flight noise to some extent. It may not, however, provide sufficient drag to stabilize a broadhead-tipped arrow for consistent accuracy.

• Decreasing arrow-shaft diameter will lessen drag in flight and improve velocity. It may improve penetration, depending on which theories you believe. Slender arrows are more difficult to fletch in general and even harder to fletch with helical. Straighter fletching does not stabilize an arrow as much as those with helical.

• Decreasing let-off and, thus, holding more draw weight will launch the arrow a few fps faster. It may be a tad harder to hold at full draw but more holding weight will allow the bowhunter to release the arrow quicker and cleaner in hunting situations.

• Decreasing string weight will improve arrow speed a bit but may make the bow noisier to shoot. Too thin of a string may not be durable enough for hunting.

• Decreasing the weight of, or eliminating, string accessories like silencers, peeps, kisser buttons, brass nock sets and string loops will allow the string to thrust forward a little faster and launch the arrow with an additional few fps. However, it will make the bow noisier and without some of these accessories, accuracy suffers.

• A looser nock fit obtained by a nock with a wider throat, thinner string or smaller center serving will

Lon shot this exceptional bull caribou with a slow, heavy aluminum arrow during a snowstorm.

launch the arrow a smidge faster. It will make less noise when nocking an arrow when hunting but if it's too loose, the arrow may fall off the string when drawing.

• Installing an overdraw-style arrow rest to shoot a shorter and lighter arrow will increase arrow speed in a similar manner as decreasing arrow weight. However, an overdraw shifts the pivot point of the arrow behind the shooter's hand/wrist. So, a more precise bow hand placement is necessary to avoid inconsistent left and right arrow impact.

• Shooting a more aerodynamically designed, lower-profile, smaller-blade or vented-blade broadhead will be easier to tune. It will be less affected by wind and may be more accurate at long range. However, expanding broadheads require more kinetic energy to get sufficient penetration and low-profile broadheads don't provide as much total cut area.

• Switching from fingers to a release aid will pick up a few fps of arrow speed because a release aid gets off the string quicker and with less friction

than fingers. However, switching from fingers to a release may require a reduction in draw length, depending on release design.

• Switching from vanes to feathers will make the arrow weigh less. Thus, out to approximately 40 yards (36 m), initial velocity will be faster but the lighter arrow will lose more momentum than a heavier, vane-fletched arrow. Plus, the textured-feather fletches will slow the arrow down more than vanes when shooting past 40 yards.

• Choosing a bow with a more radical cam or shorter brace height, or one that is more efficient at storing energy will increase arrow speed. Yet, super fast shooting bows are harder to draw smoothly when hunting. They are more critical to shoot accurately and noisier upon arrow launch.

As you can see, for everything gained there is always something lost. Determining the optimum balance between consistent accuracy in a hunting situation and maximum arrow speed is a nebulous entity. Only you can decide.

CHAPTER SEVENTEEN

The Mental Aspects of Bowhunting

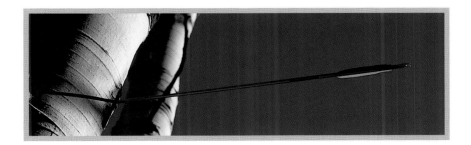

Whether you think you can make the shot on that big buck or think you can't, you're probably right. The human mind is an incredible entity capable of influencing everything you do. It all depends on whether you think positively or think with a negative slant.

Many hunts succeed or fail in the bowhunter's mind during the pursuit or perhaps just as the arrow is released. Common thoughts that will lead to disappointment include "I didn't think I could thread the arrow through the hole in the brush to make the shot," or "I didn't think I could get to the bull elk before dark," and "I shot quickly because I didn't think the deer would offer a better shot."

Conversely, some thoughts lead to bowhunting success, such as "I can and will make a good shot," or "I can stalk that bedded mule deer without being detected" and "I've been cold before; I can sit on this stand all day if that's what it takes."

Mental coaching is a huge factor—negative or positive.

Define Success

Before you can actually improve your mental game, you must first define what success means to you. Different hunters have different criteria. For example, during your first year of bowhunting, just seeing a deer or getting within bow range may be considered success. Drawing your bow in the presence of game without being detected and eventually killing a deer are also forms of bowhunting success. After twenty years of experience, perhaps only killing a record-book buck would be considered a success.

Remember, we choose bowhunting tackle to make "success" more challenging. So, equating success only with killing can set you up to fail frequently. "I could have killed that buck had I been hunting with a rifle," or "I could've easily killed a small bull today but I was holding out for a mature one," are the thoughts that help me maintain a positive mental attitude. Don't get me wrong; bringing a bowhunt to fruition by killing your quarry does fuel the flames of success. Yet putting a positive twist on every "almost" is the best way to maintain bowhunting enthusiasm necessary to keep at it day after day and year after year.

Keep a Positive Mental Attitude

The best way to succeed at anything is by having a positive mental attitude. Some people naturally have the mental capacity to turn lemons into lemonade; self-critical folks like me have to work hard at staying positive. Regardless of your nature, with diligence you can learn to be positive. In turn, success will come to all aspects where you apply positive gray matter. What you picture or think about determines, to a great deal, your success. Whatever you think a thing to be, that's what it becomes. That's how powerful your mind can be. Later in this chapter I will delve into a proven formula for developing a winning attitude.

For now, realize when it comes to bowhunting, staying positive is crucial on many levels.

• You must be positive about enduring the physical demands and weather of the hunt.

• You must stay positive so that your hunting skills will create a high-percentage shot opportunity.

• You must truly believe in your shooting abilities at the moment of truth.

The bottom line is, if you don't spend positive time in the woods, you'll never harvest game with a bow and arrow. And since it's not realistic to kill something every time afield, it's most productive to learn to appreciate the subtleties of the hunt.

Count Your Blessings

I believe it's crucial to appreciate the nuances of bowhunting—watching two young bucks sparring or just hearing the majestic bugle of a bull elk. Enjoying a solitary still hunt through the autumn woods, really clicking with a new hunting partner or simply returning home safely are forms of success, too. It's all in how you spin the thoughts in your mind on whether a particular aspect of the hunt is a success or failure.

At the end of each day, whether I'm hunting or not, I make a mental list of what I've accomplished. I use this list to motivate and keep me focused on my goals.

For example, on a recent black bear hunt in Southeast Alaska, I spent three weeks motoring around the frigid North Pacific Ocean in search of bears to stalk. When I wasn't searching for bears from a skiff, I was sitting on stand near a bait station in the rainforest swatting bugs and growing webbed feet from all the moisture! I tried everything I know to get a crack at a mature boar. Nothing seemed to work. It took nineteen days to finally kill the bear I wanted. After so much effort with no "success" it would have been easy to give up on the hunt or choke when the 7-foot (2-m) bruin presented a shot.

However, I persevered by appreciating the close calls and enjoying all the sideshows that come with the territory. I did see bears every day. I had several stalks foiled by an errant breeze. One moment I'd almost be in bow range, the next second the bear would lift its blocky head, take one sniff and vanish into the understory. I passed up several bears while on stand. Some of these encounters could have squelched my enthusiasm with a poor attitude. Yet, I used these close calls to fuel the fire.

I watched mink, marten and river otters scamper through the jungle-like rainforest, each with its own unique gait and individual hunting styles. I saw ravens dive-bombing eagles like Japanese Zeros chasing P-3s in WWII. Nature never ceases to amaze me and I'm thankful for every moment I spend afield. With a positive attitude, I turn ancillary wildlife sightings and "almosts" into success. Regardless of whether your motivators are different than mine, you should figure out what keeps your enthusiasm high and use it to your advantage.

Learn from Non-Success

Bowhunting blunders can either make you want to quit or, if viewed with the right perspective, spur you on. The first step is to stop perceiving them as failures. Stop using words like mistake or failure. Train yourself to call those instances a moment of non-success or some other affirming statement of your choice.

I'm an extremely self-critical person. I carefully scrutinize every non-success—trust me, there are plenty of them to analyze! But, I go beyond torturing myself for being a mere mortal by examining each non-success from a positive perspective. I try to learn from it and hopefully avoid the shortcoming again. For example, a lack of patience often foils otherwise effective hunting tactics. Rushing your progress on a stalk or not waiting that extra few minutes during a calling scenario often alter the outcome of a hunt.

It doesn't really matter how conspicuous of a non-success you've committed, just identify it, accept it and, most importantly, garner something positive from the experience. This pattern of thinking will eventually lead to more significant success.

Remember, the only time you should think about a problem is when creating a solution. Concentrate on what you are doing correctly. Don't dwell on blunders. The more you recall a mistake, the more it will become imprinted on your self-image and the more likely you'll talk yourself into the same error in the future.

Lon with a 450-pound black bear he killed using the spot-and-stalk method of hunting. The skull measured 20¹³⁄₁₆ inches; the hide squared at 7 feet 5 inches.

Learn from Success

Enjoying the nuances of the hunt, maintaining a positive mental attitude and spinning "almosts" in a productive manner all help with the mental aspects of bowhunting. But there's no teacher like experience. And like it or not, when bowhunting, experience means taking the life of an animal with a well-placed arrow. It's easy to point out blunders because they often make you ache with regret. However, it can be easy to over look the value of making the shot. Don't take anything for granted, pat yourself on the back and learn from the sweet moments, too. But, be aware of setting your goals too high. That can cause more damage to your confidence than you may realize.

I believe most bowhunters set standards too lofty, and, thus, pass up so-called lesser animals. Then, when they do get a crack at a trophy, they have very little experience to guide them. I think hunting magazines, books and videos frequently place unrealistic importance on trophy-caliber game and misguide the average bowhunter in the process. All bowhunters would be better served if they concentrated more on making a good shot and were less concerned about what adorns the animal's head. For me, bringing a good stalk to fruition or placing a tree stand just right that leads to a one-shot, swift kill is most pleasing. Any marginal hit or subsequent arrows shot dramatically reduces the satisfaction of the hunt for me, regardless of how big the animal was.

For the first dozen years of my bowhunting experience, I gladly killed every legal animal I could. I didn't care if it was male or female, big or small. If it was legal and within my effective range, I was flinging aluminum! Those non-trophy animals are now the solid foundation and bulk of my bowhunting experience.

Don't misinterpret; I love to get the big one as much as anyone. But I've learned to gauge success by the circumstances of the hunt as well as the trophy status of the animal. I'm quite proud of the forty-one official Pope and Young–class animals to my credit. Yet to this day, one of my most

memorable bowhunting accomplishments was killing a cow elk with my old Dynabow. It was more than twenty years ago but the event is indelibly seared into my mind's eye like a fresh brand on a heifer.

I'd spent thirteen days wading through thigh-deep snowdrifts in zero-degree temperatures to get a chance at an elk. Any elk that has survived several years of that kind of weather, plus hunting pressure, did so by being extremely cautious. So, I was elated when I stalked to within 27 yards (24.5 m) of a wary, mature cow elk in dry, crunchy snow and made a perfect shot.

Honestly, that cow elk is still in my top six all-time-favorite bow kills.

My philosophy? Don't let anyone or any preconceived notion keep you from tasting bowhunting success as frequently as possible. Disregard the arbitrary status others place on certain game animals and gain that much-needed bowhunting experience. You'll have the confidence from those harvests to maintain composure when Mr. Big walks under your stand.

Lon took this pronghorn antelope buck while hunting with Full Draw Outfitters in Colorado.

Have Confidence

Webster's Dictionary defines confidence as "the fact of being or feeling certain." That's exactly what you need regarding hunting skills and ultimately archery skills. If you are unsure of your abilities, it'll erode confidence to the point that something will go wrong.

I know both sides of the confidence issue better than I care to admit. There have been years when I was unstoppable in the hunting woods. I remember one autumn when I killed seven record-class animals and they were all one-shot kills. That confidence came from many avenues. My personal life and self-esteem were in fine order. I was extremely physically fit. And I was winning every archery tournament I entered. Thus, when any animal made the error of being close to me, I was certain of the outcome before I released an arrow.

On the other hand, I've had life challenges that crushed my confidence. During a two-year span, I endured a divorce, an office manager embezzling from me, my children moving 3,000 miles (4,800 km) away, my parents' deaths and three surgeries! During that time frame, my mental and physical readiness at crunch time was less than stellar. On countless occasions I'd do everything right as a bowhunter but then botch the shot due to a lack of concentration.

Sometimes you can't control life circumstances that affect overall confidence but you certainly have something to say about your shooting confidence. The best way to make certain you can make the shot when bowhunting is with a sound and consistent practice regimen, proper technique and a good attitude. It will also help if you rehearse making the shot in your mind.

Visualize

All the best athletes use mental imaging or visualization as a training technique to become certain of their physical tasks. Bowhunters can do the same thing.

Try fantasizing about that big buck padding down the trail past your stand. Then visualize how he stops at the mock scrape and paws the rut-scented dirt. When his near front leg moves forward to expose his vitals and his head bobs behind that extended leg so it obscures his vision, you draw and anchor subconsciously. Muscle memory takes over and the only conscious thought is picking a spot and you aim, aim, aim. The shot goes off and you visualize the arrow hitting exactly where you were certain it would go.

Make sure you visualize every little detail and rehearse it often. Make up various hunting scenarios. Live them out in your mind. Not only does this tactic keep your mind busy during hunting lulls, it's amazing how the mind can convince the body to perform flawlessly at crunch time.

Target Panic and Buck Fever

When shooting at targets, it's called "target panic." When hunting it's called "buck fever." Whatever you call it, this frustrating experience affects most archers and bowhunters to some degree. Whether they admit the problem and address it properly is an entirely different matter.

This ailment manifests itself in so many forms it can be difficult to quantify. In general, target panic or buck fever involves any number of symptoms:

• uncontrollable shaking

• snap shooting

• drive-by shooting

• gunching the release

• plucking the string

• freezing the sight picture off target

• not picking a spot causing you to shoot at the entire animal instead of a specific aiming location

• flinching

• pushing the bow upon release

• other mental errors that cause a breakdown in shooting effectively.

Target Panic

For years, I could not hold my sight pin in the bull's-eye. I would come to full draw, anchor, let the sight pin drift down through the spot, then was unable to lift the bow, as if it weighed 1,000 pounds (450 kg), to get the pin back into the center of the bull's-eye. I'd literally bounce the bow up and down ever so slightly and then try to time the release when the pin was closest to the spot!

Lon made a good, one-shot kill on this Pope and Young–class Sitka black-tailed buck on Kodiak Island.

Sound familiar? I even adjusted my sights so when I held at six o'clock on the bull's-eye, the arrow would actually impact higher and, thus, into the spot. This worked for a while. Then I would start anticipating my pin getting close to the bottom of the spot and would freeze below where I knew the pin must be to make an accurate shot. Now that's target panic!

Buck Fever

One fall I hunted my fanny off in Nevada for mule deer followed by another arduous hunt for Columbia blacktails in northern California.

After twenty days of hunting, I had nothing to show for my efforts except weary bones. Then, on the 17-mile (27-km) hike out of the mountains, a "dorky forky" blacktail stood barely 20 yards (18 m) away and gawked. I was so excited to finally get a shot and perhaps redeem myself as a "worthy" hunter that I barely had the strength to draw my bow. Once at full draw, I was so anxious and afraid the young buck might run off that I didn't aim effectively and shot way too quickly.

I missed so badly it didn't even scare the buck. My hunting buddy thought I missed intentionally! I quickly nocked another arrow and proceeded to miss a second shot when the deer was just 25 yards (23 m) away. The juvenile deer trotted out to 50 yards (45.5 m) and stopped again.

I distinctly recall mentally coaching myself. "This is ridiculous, calm down, pick a spot and follow through." My body did as my mind instructed and I dotted that buck at 50 yards. He only went 15 paces before collapsing.

How can an experienced bowhunter and nine-time state archery champion miss a small buck at 20 and 25 yards (18 and 23 m) and then make a perfect shot at 50 yards (45.5 m)? It's called buck fever. I was just too desperate and so anxious that my shooting skills turned to mush. The more important the shot, the more likely you will try too hard, won't relax, your mind short-circuits and your body fails to perform.

To further explain this exasperating affliction I'll

use an example Bernie Pellerite shared with me. He asked, "What's the difference between walking on a 2x12-inch (5x30-cm) board laid flat on the floor and walking on that same plank when it's 50 feet (15 m) in the air?" Of course, the only difference is the fear of falling off the board when it's elevated. Otherwise, you would put one foot in front of the other and walk like you've done all your life. It's that fear of falling or, in the case of buck fever, the fear of missing or the fear of "failing" that causes the self-induced pressure. You must trust your shot sequence regardless of how far or how important the target. Of course, the more consistent your shot sequence, the better the results and, thus, the easier to trust.

Another common symptom of buck fever is a dramatic loss of memory. I can't count the times I've watched hunting buddies shoot at game and not recall the details of the event. One time a friend shot at a buck five times before connecting with the extraordinarily curious deer. I watched and counted as the scenario unfolded. When I approached him and the dandy buck, I first congratulated him and then teased him about shooting five times. He vehemently denied shooting that many arrows. Only when I suggested he count the remaining arrows in his quiver and do some simple math did he believe he had shot five times.

Buck fever frequently makes you so desperate for "success" that you also forget simple aspects of your shooting routine—like picking a spot. I'm convinced this form of buck fever is the most common affliction. One of my most painful and, thus, meaningful cases of buck fever occurred early in my bowhunting tenure.

I was hunting elk in the high country of Colorado when I intercepted a large herd of elk moving across a steep-sided, sparsely forested ridge. The scene reminded me of a shooting gallery at a carnival. Instead of little metal ducks tracking around in an endless circle with carnival music in the background, streams of elk filtered by in what seemed like unending waves with bulls bugling everywhere. Even though this event occurred more than twenty years ago, the vision is etched in my mind.

Finally, a spike bull stopped broadside, directly below my rocky bench. At the time, I could hit a paper plate

at 60 yards (55 m) every time in practice so I didn't hesitate to take a 45-yard (41-m) shot at an elk with a kill zone the size of a beach ball. I promptly aimed with the 40-yard (36-m) pin high on his body, the 50-yard (45.5-m) pin low on his body. I shot with good form and the arrow flew true to its mark.

Unfortunately, I had not picked a spot. I had virtually shot at the entire elk. I can still see the sight picture in my mind. The tip of my pins were aligned with the bull's hindquarter—not in the crease of his front shoulder. The arrow hit the elk square in the ham.

Luckily for both of us, the broadhead hit the elk's femur, stopping the arrow cold. With only a few inches (centimeters) of penetration and the arrow falling out almost immediately, the bull endured much less trauma than if he'd been jousted by an antler. I watched him run down the mountain and up the other side as if nothing had happened. In spite of an exhaustive search, there was no blood on the ground and no elk to be found.

I'm certain the bull recovered fully. Even so, this event upset me. I have great reverence for my quarry and never intentionally shoot for anything but the vitals. I then realized just how important it is to pick a spot.

A bull's-eye target has a distinct aiming spot that forces you to concentrate. Not so with game animals. You must consciously and visually select a small, specific aiming locale. It takes incredible concentration to narrow your focus from the entire animal down to a quarter-size spot. Without that level of fine aiming, you will not achieve fine results! Hopefully these examples will clarify buck fever and target panic so you can identify your particular afflictions.

Admit the Problem

Some folks may feel embarrassed to admit they get buck fever or can't hold on the spot in practice. However, the first step toward improving any ailment is to recognize and admit the problem. "Hello, my name is Lon Lauber. I have target panic and buck fever!" Once you've admitted the problem you must commit to improving in your particular areas of weakness. There are almost as many ways to combat buck fever as there are symptoms. However, there are a select few antidotes that seem to help most people.

Proven Antidotes

Without question, the most effective antidotes for buck fever and target panic are positive experiences that bolster confidence. The more times you've been able to pick a spot and maintain composure while shooting at game that leads to a quick, humane kill, the more likely you will be able to do so on a regular basis. The more frequently you believe you can make the shot under tournament pressure and actually do, the more likely it will become a common occurrence.

That's why I strongly recommend all bowhunters lower their "trophy" standards until they have enough experience in bowhunting and shooting at game to keep buck fever in check most of the time. Granted, you should become excited in the presence of game. It's primal instinct to get a rush of adrenaline. However, it's counterproductive to get so jacked up you can't perform anywhere near your capabilities. Self-talk or mental coaching at the moment of truth is very effective. Learn to mentally talk yourself through the pressure situations. Also, you'll get the best results if you stay focused on the procedure of the shot and don't even think about the outcome.

As to target panic, I have it under control by shooting with back tension to cause a surprise release. In a nutshell, here's the technique for achieving that, which is covered in more detail in Chapters 7 and 8.

1. Start with a close, generic backstop.

2. Shoot with eyes closed until you learn the feel of good shooting form.

3. Open your eyes but don't add sights or a target just yet. Learn to see and feel a good surprise release.

4. Add a sight and repeat the process.

5. Add a very large bull's-eye, such as a paper plate. Shoot from just a few feet; learn to let the pin or sight picture float around in the spot.

6. Slowly reduce the size of the aiming spot and increase the distance.

If at any time you start to feel anxious or revert to old, bad habits like punching the trigger or freezing below the spot, move closer and use a larger aiming spot.

It takes about 2,000 shots just to begin turning the new technique into habit. It may take several months to get it right.

Taming target panic to the point of it being a non-issue will greatly reduce problems with buck fever as well. I'm certain the more confident you become with shooting skills in practice, the more confident you will become when shooting at game. Remember, if you think you can make the shot, you will. If you doubt your abilities, you'll probably miss. Practice and gain confidence by making every lesson a positive one.

Here's Lon with his Pope and Young–class brown bear.

The following tips to improve your mental game are used with permission from Lanny Bassham, Olympic shooting medalist and the author of *With Winning in Mind.*

• If fear of missing or failure causes you problems, you need more experience.

• If becoming too excited is the aliment, learn to think positively. Use self-talk like, "I can and will make the shot!" Visualize performing well. Sometimes even yawning can help calm nerves in a pressure situation.

• Consistent and effective performance is a balanced combination of your conscious mind, your subconscious mind and your self-image.

• The *conscious mind* is the part of the brain that holds your thoughts and memory. This is where you set goals, think or generate thoughts and where self-talk occurs. The conscious mind is the source of your thoughts and mental pictures. It controls all of the senses: seeing, hearing, smelling, tasting and touching. It is what you picture or think about.

• The *subconscious mind* is what controls all the things you do without having to think about them like walking, talking, driving, shooting a bow with a surprise release and other skills or techniques. The subconscious mind is the source of your skills and power to perform. All great performances are accomplished subconsciously. We develop skill through repetition of conscious thought until it becomes automatically performed by the subconscious mind.

• The *self-image* is what makes you act like you. It is the total of your habits and your attitudes. Your performance always equals your self-image. "I can and will make the shot" is an example of self-image.

• What you picture or think about determines, to a great deal, your success. So, think about and visualize making the shot. Whatever you think a thing to be, that's what it becomes. It's important to keep the three aspects of your mind in balance. Imagine the conscious mind, subconscious mind and self-image as equal-sized and overlapping circles in complete balance.

This is called the *Triad State*, which is learning to keep the conscious circle, subconscious circle and self-image circle in harmony and balance. If any of the three elements become too powerful or too weak, your results will suffer.

Here are some suggestions on building each of the three circles:

Building the Conscious Circle. When you really need to make the shot, relax and enjoy the moment. Keep your mind on the process, not the outcome. Think about, talk about and write about only what you want to happen with the shot. To improve your chance of success, rehearse often making the shot in your mind (visualize). And, don't try too hard. Just follow your shot sequence just as you've done a thousand times in practice.

Building the Subconscious Circle. Effective training and practice allow more aspects of the shot to become subconscious. Remember, practice does not make perfect. Perfect practice makes perfect. Try focusing only on what you are doing correctly in practice. Disregard the negative aspects. Train and practice with shooters more skilled than you are. This will encourage you to rise to the occasion.

Building the Self-Image Circle. Use terms like "hit" and "non-hit" instead of hit and miss. When scoring, use terms like "ten" and "non-ten." When it comes to tournament results, refer to your accomplishments as "wins" and "attempts to win." In all aspects strive to imprint positive results only. A good way to build a positive self-image is to transfer successful self-images in other areas of your life to shooting a bow or to bowhunting success. For example, I have the utmost confidence in making great photos. So I imagine making the shot with bow and arrow to be as easy as it is for me to make a great photo.

The Conscious Mind

The Sub-Conscious Mind

The Self-Image

CHAPTER EIGHTEEN

Shooting in Adverse Conditions

Some of the best bowhunting opportunities occur in the worst weather and most unfriendly terrain. In my experience, most big-game species seem to let their guard down in crummy weather.

There's one exception: I've seen whitetails act especially nervous on windy days. The wind masks the movement and noise a predator would make. The deer can't be sure if what it saw or heard is truly dangerous. In general though, it seems most game animals' senses are less accurate when it's raining, snowing, windy or foggy. Or, maybe they are more concerned with surviving the bad weather than avoiding predators? Regardless of the reason, they are less cautious and more huntable.

Moreover, foul weather is a frequent catalyst to spur on the rut. I can't count the number of times I've seen a dramatic dip in temperature or a good snowfall increase rut behavior—with many different species. Also, steep, rugged terrain frequently allows a bowhunter to approach game animals undetected. Unfortunately, the same nasty weather or steep terrain that creates close proximity to your quarry are the same conditions that make shooting a bow even more challenging. Thus, once you have your bow tuned, sighted in and shooting well, most of your practice should be in hunting-like scenarios.

Steep Angles

The most common adverse condition a bowhunter will face is shooting at a steep angle. Since most bowhunting occurs from an elevated tree stand, learning to shoot effectively on a downward slope is crucial to success.

There are two key components to shooting accurately at severe angles. One, it's important to

maintain the T-shape torso aspect of your shooting form by bending at the waist. However, it's not conducive in a hunting scenario to draw your bow on the level and then, like a robot, bend at the waist to achieve the proper shooting angle. This extra movement may spook your target animal. Through conscious practice you must learn to draw from a bent angle, yet still maintain proper form from the waist up.

Two, gravity only affects the arrow's trajectory across the horizontal distance it travels—not the angled distance. For example, if your bow launches an arrow at 240 fps (73 mps) and you were shooting downward at a deer from a 30-degree angle from a tree stand and your range finder indicated the deer was 47 yards (43 m) away, you'd aim dead-on with the 40-yard (36-m) pin that was sighted in on flat ground. If you were to aim on this angled shot as if it were a 47-yard shot on flat terrain, your arrow would impact so high you'd miss the deer completely!

Remember, the steeper the angle, the farther your target animal and the slower your arrow flies, the more you'll have to compensate to make a vital hit. Also, you must aim a little low when shooting on steep, upward angles, too, although you don't have to compensate quite as much on the same angle shooting uphill as you do shooting downhill.

You may scoff at the mathematical reality because you've shot many whitetails from an elevated stand and never compensated at all and still killed them. There are several contributing factors to explain this contradiction. Perhaps you shoot a relatively fast arrow and, thus, in the excitement of the hunt, you don't notice the arrow impacting a little higher than where you aimed. Also, at angles less than 20 degrees and shots closer than 20 yards (18 m), the difference in trajectory will be slight. This is especially true since the average deer has vitals equivalent to an 8-inch (20-cm) paper plate. This vertical window of error will keep your arrow in the deer's kill zone even though you misaimed by several yards (meters).

Since every arrow velocity, every angle and every distance requires a different amount of compensation—whether shooting downhill or uphill—it's impossible for me to provide data for all situations. Once again, practicing with your hunting tackle in a manner similar to the way you'll be hunting is critical to making the shot. The following personal experience is a good example of this point.

One year I belonged to three archery leagues and, between practices and tournaments, was shooting almost every weekend. Not only was I shooting well, I had my arrow's trajectory figured out. I knew just how much to compensate when shooting at steep angles, where to aim when lofting an arrow over a branch and into the vitals of a distant 3-D target and so on.

Then, a month prior to a Sitka blacktail hunt, I changed my worn-out bowstring. In the process of

re-tuning that once-familiar bow, I severely strained my bow-pulling muscles. I laid off shooting for three weeks to let the muscles heal. Then, just a week before the hunt, I tried shooting again. I couldn't even pull my bow! So, I backed off the poundage by 10 pounds (4.5 kg) and switched to a heavier, yet weaker-spined, arrow to achieve good arrow flight. I was able to get the bow tuned and sighted in just in time for the hunt. In my haste, however, I didn't shoot the new setup at steep angles or at point-blank range.

In the first few days of the trip, I missed three Pope and Young bucks at less than 20 yards (18 m)! The new setup created a more arching trajectory than what I was used to. In the steep terrain blacktails call home, I zipped arrows right over the back of those bucks. When it happened twice in the same day, I was so disgusted I almost tossed the bow down the mountain. Instead, I swore if I got another close, steep shot, I'd compensate by aiming particularly low. I could live with a low miss but I wasn't going to shoot over another deer. So, I kept hunting.

That evening, just before dark, about 5 miles (8 km) from camp, I grunted in the biggest Sitka buck I've ever seen. When the rut-crazed deer stopped broadside at 13 yards (12 m), I recall coaching myself to aim low. I intentionally aimed my 20-yard (18-m) pin below his brisket and in line with his knee. The slow, arching arrow blew through the center of the buck's chest.

Just a little attentive practice before the hunt at close range and steep angles would have shown I needed to hold several inches (cm) low on such a shot. But then again, this lesson may not have had the same impact, and I may have been "tagged-out" before getting that big buck.

If the downhill-angled distance is 99 yards, shoot for 60 yards.
-50°

If the uphill-angled distance is 87.7 yards, shoot for 60 yards.
+50°

At the same 50° angle, if the downhill distance is 65 yards, shoot for 40 yards; for 32 yards angled distance, shoot for 20 yards.

At the same 50° angle, if the uphill distance is 60 yards, shoot for 40 yards; for 31 yards angled distance, shoot for 20 yards.

The acceleration of gravity slows down the upward velocity of the arrow when it is shot uphill and speeds up the arrow's velocity when it is shot downhill. Thus, an arrow leaving the bow at 240 fps (73 mps) will travel 87.7 yards (80 m) in 1.1 seconds when shot at a 50° uphill angle whereas the same arrow would travel 99 yards (90 m) in 1.1 seconds at a 50° downhill angle.

Side Slopes

Besides compensating for steep angles, be aware of what frequently happens when shooting on side slopes. Gravity's effect will frequently trick you into believing you are holding your bow level or perpendicular to the ground, but you really have the bow canted. This will cause left or right misses—depending on whether it's a left-facing or right- facing slope. To actually hold your bow level it will feel like you are pushing or twisting the top wheel of your bow into the uphill side of the slope.

The next time you are shooting on a roving course, pay attention to those targets located on a side slope. I promise the majority of the arrow holes will be located on the downhill side of the bull's-eye.

The best way to shoot straight on side-sloping terrain is to use a bow sight with a bubble level. Unfortunately it's not as simple as just slapping one onto your bow. First, you should check to ensure the sight's level is plumb when your bow riser is plumb. You can use a predetermined plumb object like a doorjamb to see if the bow's riser is in synch with the sight's bubble. Some sights have adjustments for this. Others may have to be shimmed between the sight bracket and the riser so the bubble and the bow coincide. The R.S. Bow Vise and R.S. String Level make this chore a snap.

Furthermore, to get the best results with a bow level, you must check how the level reads when the bow is at full draw when shooting on steep uphill and downhill angles. The bow riser may twist under tension when the wheels roll over and transfer the load from the string side to the cable side of the cam. The cable guard pulling the string out of the arrow's path also creates some sideways torque on the riser.

These things can actually make a bubble level lie—even if it reads true when the bow is static and/or shooting on level ground. The cure for this is to hang a string with a weight from a tall wall. (The weight will automatically plumb the string.) Then, while at full draw, check the bubble's accuracy when aiming on steep upward and downward angles. This is called "leveling the third axis" of the sight. If you do a lot of long-range, steep-angle shooting, a sight with a third-axis-leveling adjustment would be a wise purchase.

Awkward Positions

If compensating for steep angles and slide slopes isn't enough, bowhunters must often shoot from an awkward stance. A perfect example is shooting my best mule deer to date: I was straddling a crevasse in a rock cliff. I had to shoot straight down with the bow between my spread legs and the arrow had to thread through a hole in the brush the size of a tennis ball. Now that's a shot you just don't practice very often!

Weird stances when bowhunting are almost always more common than your normal practice stance. Bowhunter leagues, hunter-oriented 3-D shoots and stump shooting with friends are the best practice to learn how to shoot from the various and uncomfortable positions common to bowhunting scenarios.

Another example comes from my experience shooting a mountain goat in the Kenai Mountains: It was so steep, I was sitting on my rump and feet spread apart with heels digging into the loose rock cliff. My bow was between my legs and, while at full draw, I had to check to make sure the lower cam rolling over would not smash into rocks upon the shot. I didn't have to thread the arrow through a hole in brush but the wind was gusting about 30 miles per hour (48 kmph). Even at 20 yards (18 m), I barely made the shot.

Wind

Sometimes, the same breeze that belies your presence is the one that makes aiming a very nerve-wracking event. Once, on a Colorado mule deer hunt, I stalked a dandy buck and got within 30 yards (27 m) of him because the prairie wind disguised my approach quite well. Unfortunately, when compensating for the strong wind gusts, I aimed to the side of the deer. Just as I released, the wind stopped and my arrow whizzed past him right where I'd been aiming! Needless to say, shooting an arrow in windy conditions is a tricky proposition. Fortunately, if you know you'll be hunting in windy conditions, there are a few things you can do to improve your chances.

Slender arrows with a low-profile broadhead and smaller fletches create less surface area. Thus, they are less affected by the wind. A faster arrow has less time between you and the target animal to be pushed off course. For example, it takes an arrow leaving the bow at 200 fps (61 mps) about 1 second to cover 60 yards (55 m). An arrow zipping out of the bow at 300 fps (91 mps) will impact the target animal in about 0.6 second. That's 40 percent less time for the arrow to drift in the wind.

Practice is always the best teacher. Arrow surface area and velocity, wind direction and its speed will vary with every shot scenario. The best way to shoot in the wind is to aim off target by the distance you think the arrow will drift, and release with a controlled punch. This is one of two scenarios when I don't advocate shooting with a surprise release. (The other is when an animal is moving and stopping at unpredictable intervals, such as when a rutting buck is chasing a doe. He may not be standing there five seconds later. Thus, a quick release is required.)

Other things to consider when shooting in the

wind are not shooting at all or getting so close the wind has very little time to affect the arrow. That's exactly what I did when shooting a Kodiak caribou.

I was still-hunting on the leeward side of a knife-edge ridge (mostly to stay out of the 60 mph/97 kmph gusts that were creating a windchill of −30˚F/−34˚C). Lucky for me, the band of caribou was munching lichens on the windward side of the ridge.

I found a level slab of volcanic rock just barely the size of my boots. While waiting, one of the animals approached and stood on the apex a mere 7 yards (6.4 m) from me. Since I had stable footing, could aim without the wind's effect and the arrow only had to travel a few feet (meters) exposed to the wind, I cut the shot.

I saw the arrow wag sideways when it cleared the ridge. Happily, it straightened out and hit the caribou within a couple inches (few centimeters) of where I was aiming.

Rain and Wet Weather

It's not much fun, but prudent practice to shoot in wet, rainy conditions. There's much to learn about your equipment in damp conditions. Because of my tenure in Alaska, I've killed a pile of animals when it was raining. I've also had the rain spoil several shot opportunities. Some things to consider are: How does shooting in a raincoat affect your form? Will the bulk of the raingear cause string interference? Will your gloved hand create a different feel on the bow handle and will that change the arrow's point of impact? Will a wet release or tab shoot differently?

As with the wind, the direction and density of rainfall will dictate how much you have to compensate your aim. In a light drizzle I would not compensate at all. During a moderate rain I'd aim just a tad into the rain. If the rain were pouring, I'd consider not shooting at all—the downpour may push the arrow off course substantially and it certainly will wash away the blood trail.

Another thing to consider is bow and arrow maintenance in wet weather. Keeping feathers aloft in the rain is difficult yet vital to accurate shooting. I always hunt with vane-fletched arrows in sloppy conditions so I don't have to fuss with feathers.

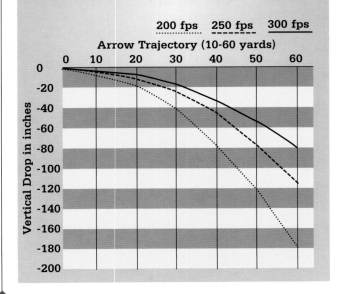

UNDERSTANDING ARROW TRAJECTORY

Arrow trajectory is influenced by many factors: initial arrow launch velocity, arrow weight, aerodynamic "drag" (which is affected by the size, shape and texture of the arrow, fletching and broadhead) and the arrow's front of center (FOC) balance point.

The graph below is based on a 29-inch-long, 400-grain arrow with an outside diameter of 0.35 inch and three, four-inch vanes that are 0.5 inch tall. The only variable is the initial arrow velocity (200, 250 and 300 fps).

As you can see, precise yardage estimation and critical aiming are needed to achieve proper shot placement into the paper-plate-size vitals of a deer—especially at longer yardages.

200 fps   250 fps   300 fps

Arrow Trajectory (10-60 yards)

However, if you are a staunch feather fan, there are several products made to weatherproof those wilting fletches. You can also enclose the feathers in a plastic bag to ward off rain.

Additionally, damp weather can wreak havoc on moving bow parts and fog optics, and generally make a mess of everything. This is especially true when hunting near saltwater. The corrosion can cause cable guards to squeak, and other moving parts to rust or even seize if left unchecked. Keep your tackle as clean and dry as possible.

The smallest oversight can cause the biggest problem. For example, a rain-clogged peep can throw you off kilter just long enough to squander the shot opportunity.

One time I was dogging a lustful bruiser of a buck in a heavy rain. After a couple hours of literally chasing him, I managed to get above and in front of him. When he walked out into the open, stopped, looked the other way and moved his near front leg forward, I had alreaady mentally tagged him before I even drew my bow.

When I did, the sight picture was blurry and I was confused. By the time I let down, shook the rain out of the peep and drew again, the buck had walked off without even realizing I was nearby.

Now, when a shot opportunity is close at hand, I check the peep for rain or snow. If for some reason I don't notice the clogged peep until I'm at full draw, I lower the peep to my mouth and suck in the moisture. This is much quieter than blowing on the clogged peep.

Snow and Freezing Temperatures

When the temperature drops and rain turns to snow, you have a different set of concerns that may botch the shot.

One frozen morning when hunting moose, I had a beautiful, wide-racked bull come right in to my partner's seductive cow moose moans. Before I knew it, the bull was broadside at 35 yards (32 m) and offering a good shot. So I took it. Unfortun-ately, my arrow was encased with ice lumps that steered my arrow off course by several feet! Had I just taken a few seconds to run my gloved hand up and down to clean the arrow shaft before nocking the arrow....

So it goes with all your archery tackle. Make sure all moving parts are functioning properly and there's no ice buildup on the string, cams, arrows, rest, sight, peep, release, etc.

Another problem to avoid occurs when it rains and then freezes. A fleece-covered arrow-rest launcher arm will freeze to the fleece-covered riser shelf like it was glued! And broadheads can freeze into the foam of a quiver hood like they were set in cement. The bottom line is, you must check and keep checking the functionality of your bow rig when it's snowing and below freezing.

Moreover, the additional clothes needed to stay warm in nippy temperatures will frequently alter shooting form enough to change the arrow's point of impact a few inches (centimeters) at 20 yards (18 m) and more at longer distances. One time I was so frozen I couldn't even draw my bow when a Pope and Young whitetail stopped 16 yards (14.5 m) from my lofty perch. I think shooting 5 or even 10 pounds (2.25 or 4.5 kg) less draw weight and a 1/2-inch-shorter (12-mm) draw length in arctic conditions is very prudent. At the very least, employing heat packs and drawing your bow frequently on stand to keep limber are paramount.

Hot Weather

On the other end of the weather spectrum is hot and dry or hot and humid weather. Don't leave your bow in a hot, locked car. The string may creep (permanently elongate) and/or the peep will rotate, changing your sight picture or causing a change in the arrow's point of impact. When it's really hot in a closed vehicle, the bow's limbs may delaminate. Having your bow explode will end the hunt abruptly.

Sand, dust or grit can cause a game-spooking chatter when drawing the bow. Just ask my good friend, Rich Eckles. He made a great stalk on a monster caribou only to have the bull dash away when it heard a violin-like screech when he came to full draw. Cleaning the arrow and running a finger over the arrow rest prior to drawing would have made the difference.

The cable slide and other moving parts can sing at the wrong time, too, if you're not careful. Be aware that a waxed string or heavily oiled moving parts will attract dust and grit like iron filings to a magnet. Check all moving parts before the moment of truth.

CHAPTER NINETEEN

Moment of Truth—Shooting Big Game

Being a good hunter isn't enough. To score time and again, you must know when and where to shoot—and maintain composure at "crunch time."

Crunch time is when the success of the entire hunt is riding on a few moments. You have to make quick, precise decisions. Furthermore, your mind has to sufficiently control your body to perform the task at hand—slowly drawing a bow and shooting accurately. This may sound easy while reading, but any bowhunter who's been within spittin' distance of game knows how emotionally overwhelming crunch time can be.

When and where to shoot and crunch time are the challenges of bowhunting, because they make you deal with three situations nearly simultaneously:

First, when bowhunting, being close to your quarry is paramount. While it increases odds for a humane harvest, it also complicates the situation; you must draw undetected so as not to spook the game. Considering most big-game animals have outstanding movement perception, this is no small order.

Second, due to the manner in which an arrow kills, the body position of the target animal is also crucial.

Third, anxiousness and lack of confidence usually cause mental errors at crunch time.

The following are some suggestions that may help you make good decisions in these situations.

When to Shoot

Take a recent bowhunting non-success of mine as an example of what not to do....

While hunting cougar-skittish Columbian black-tailed deer in a remote wilderness, my buddy and I located a bachelor group of mature bucks. One was a monster whose antlers were so large that any mule deer would've worn them proudly. It was too late in the day to make a move. But the next morning found me slipper-footing my way into bow range on three other dandy bucks. Mr. Monster wasn't around—or so I thought.

Having an arrow nocked and ready while easing down on the unsuspecting trio, I inadvertently jumped Mr. Monster from his timber-thick bed. He bounced down between the giant Douglas firs and stopped in the open! Fir boughs blocked my shooting lane so I carefully sidestepped three times. With the buck slightly quartering, and looking back up at me, I drew slowly and then quickly cut the shot. The arrow harmlessly whizzed by the buck. He vanished with his life and huge velvet-adorned antlers intact.

Instantly, I knew my mistake. I shot way too fast and plucked the string. That's why I shot to the right. If he had stood there long enough for me to sidestep three paces and draw a bow, I certainly had time to execute good form, too! In hindsight, it's obvious the buck wasn't overly alarmed. Taking a few extra seconds during the shot sequence certainly was in order.

I'm still chapped about missing that trophy buck. However, it solidified an important aspect of my crunch-time philosophy: If an animal isn't going to stand long enough to execute good shooting form, then I shouldn't be shooting.

I've beat myself up over this one plenty. But, critically analyzing each mistake or success has helped me grow as a bowhunter.

Anticipate Behavior

Like a card shark, a bowhunter must make decisive, confident decisions and, at the same time, anticipate and predict the opponent's next move. I'm convinced those who are familiar with wildlife behavior are more successful bowhunters. Of course, field experience is the best teacher, but you can study photos and determine what the animal was doing at the time of exposure. Better yet, watch nature shows and hunting videos, or go to an animal enclosure. The idea is to anticipate the creature's next move. Ask yourself, "When could I draw my bow without being detected?"

For me, photographing wildlife has been a tremendous help. Even with a telephoto lens, camera range and bow range are similar. Furthermore, anticipating what a mammal will do next enables me to capture a variety of behavior on film.

Another suggestion is to start shooting interactive computer/video archery games. They're great fun. From an educational standpoint, they force you to wait for the right shot. Then the system records your arrow's point of impact as a kill, wound or miss. These video games aren't perfect but they are good training aids.

While all these suggestions help, nothing can replace actually killing an animal with archery tackle.

Window of Opportunity

Foam targets don't move so we are methodical in practice. When an animal presents even the slightest opportunity, however, we often rush and take a haphazard shot as I did with that giant blacktail. Learning when to draw and shoot during that window of opportunity is the key.

To unlock that window, it's important to realize that each species (and, for that matter, each individual animal) has its own tolerance to human presence, sound or movement. On a broad spectrum, whitetails are not very tolerant of movement. Those whitetails that stood around after picking up strange movement are dead. At the other end, moose are mostly wilderness creatures with little human predator experience, so they are more likely to gawk before running. Learning your target animal's survival tactics will help determine when to shoot.

To further illustrate this point, I'll use my Alaska deer hunting experience as reference. In a five-year span, I legally killed sixteen Sitka blacktail bucks. Of these, five were totally aware of my presence. They just watched me shoot them. Six had seen movement but hadn't determined its origin as danger. Five bucks had no clue to their impending demise. On closer scrutiny, this unspooky behavior can be explained because in most places, Sitkas

seldom encounter man, and by nature they are quite curious. Also, my hunts mostly occurred during the rut, which played a strong role in distracting these deer from sensing my presence as danger.

Contrast this with my whitetail experience. In the past three years I've killed two decent bucks. Each of many times when a whitetail noticed my presence, it fled. My point is, Sitka blacktails are generally more tolerant of movement while preparing to shoot. With whitetails, if you don't wait for the perfect time to draw, you won't ever kill one.

This principle holds true with all species. You just have to learn what individuals of each species will tolerate in a given situation. This is no small task.

The closer you are, the more likely an animal will spook from movement and sound. You have to determine an appropriate time and distance to shoot. Of course, if you can draw and shoot when the animal is totally unaware, this is ideal. Wait for them to feed, turn and look away, or their eyes to become obstructed. Beware though; even with their head down, most herbivores (which have eyes on the sides of the head) can pick up movement almost behind them. If you can see any part of their eye, they can probably see you!

I was painfully reminded of this while hunting Dall sheep.

I had spent six days trying to get a shot. Each day resulted in an "almost." Then one evening three rams fed over a steep, benchlike ridge. I circled up and around the mountain and still-hunted down the benches. I fully expected to see the sheep just over each ledge.

Finally, I caught a glimpse. A rocky ledge obstructed the white ram's vision. It was almost perfect—but due to the steepness, I had precarious footing. Since the ram was unaware, I eased forward to better footing. Once, the ram scanned for danger. I froze. He then continued feeding. My trophy ram was slightly quartering away at 25 yards (23 m). Unfortunately, he bolted while I was drawing my bow.

Later, I realized he'd sensed something wrong when scanning but continued feeding while watching out of the "back of his eyes." Had I waited ten or fifteen seconds after he put his head back down, I would have been okay.

Fortunately, two days later, I had another opportunity on a Dall ram. This time, I stalked and waited for the perfect time to draw. The next day I was packing-out a top-ranked Pope and Young ram. Once again, timing and minimal movement proved necessary to succeed.

Distractions

Sometimes you are more likely to get away with sound or movement than other times. Animals are usually more skittish on windy days, even though it's harder for them to discern movement from that of wind-blown vegetation. Also, animals miss some details when moving. This is why retrievers are trained to sit until the bird is down before fetching. Dogs can visually locate a downed bird much better when still. They aren't as effective if they take off while the bird is falling. In many bowhunting scenarios, I've been able to slowly rearrange myself when an animal is approaching. Still it's best not to move unless you can't see their eyes.

The most lenient time for movement is when rattling, calling and/or decoying. You have to consider the animal's mindset when using these tactics. If a rutting buck hears antlers clicking together and he comes to investigate, his eyes are fully expecting to find two bucks sparring. Thus, some movement would be natural. Learning to draw a bow slowly pays off. With a molasses-like slow motion, you can sometimes shoot before a buck determines the movement's origin.

Another type of distraction to consider is sound. Try releasing your arrow in synchronization with some distracting sound. Frequently, this will beat the string-jumping problem. These sounds could be rustling leaves caused by the wind or another animal approaching. Try shooting when the animal is eating or bugling, for example. In rural hunting areas consider manmade sounds like cars, trains or even barking dogs to muffle your shot.

One more distraction to be aware of is "invisible brush." Small twigs and branches tend to disappear when concentrating on your quarry. Participating in 3-D shoots has helped me look for these shot spoilers. Now, out of habit, I automatically check for arrow deflectors before I even think about drawing.

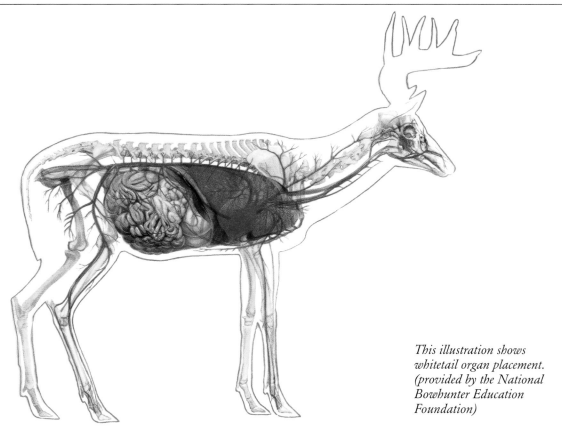

This illustration shows whitetail organ placement. (provided by the National Bowhunter Education Foundation)

Where to Shoot

Determining when to shoot is a lifelong learning process. Where to shoot is simple:

• If you can't make a razor-sharp broadhead penetrate the vitals, don't shoot.

• A heart shot is great but too small a target to intentionally shoot for.

• Liver hits are lethal but it may take longer for the animal to succumb.

• A double-lung hit is best. The animal expires almost instantly.

Remember, we frequently choose archery tackle to make success more challenging. It's okay not to kill every time an animal is in bow range. I prefer passing up marginal shots to taking iffy shots and spending all day anxiously trailing a poorly hit animal. I hope you do, too.

But let's not kid anyone here, I don't always make a perfect double-lung hit. However, I never shoot an arrow without fully intending to hit both lungs. Sometimes things do go wrong. Maybe I've misjudged distance and hit a little high or low. Perhaps the animal takes a step just as I release. Regardless of the situation, my intent is to always get both lungs.

Angles

In my opinion, problems occur when bowhunters force a situation by taking angled shots of low percentage. There are many angles appropriate for a rifle but not a bow. Even if you shoot like Robin Hood it's just not wise to take frontal or steeply angled shots.

With frontal shots, there are too many bones and too small of a window into the vitals. On front-quartering shots, an arrow risks hitting heavy shoulder bones or only one lung. Hitting one lung is usually but not always lethal. The run time on a single-lung hit is greater. This could reduce the chance of recovery.

Steep, rear-quartering shots greatly increase the odds of an arrow deflecting off ribs. This puts the broadhead into the animal's armpit and not vital tissue. Furthermore, an arrow shot from a steep rear-quartering angle may only catch one lung or lose momentum in the paunch before reaching the vitals.

The National Bowhunter Education Foundation has great anatomical charts and models. It's your responsibility to know where a particular animal's bone structure lies in comparison to its vitals. For instance, you'll learn that for most broadside shots, you should shoot close to the shoulder crease and one-third the way up from the brisket.

Calling the Shot

Similar to billiards, I find it's challenging and educational to call the shot. After shooting an animal and before recovery, try predicting where and what the arrow hit. In just a few minutes, upon recovery, you can see where the arrow entered, what tissue damage occurred and where the arrow exited. A few extra minutes here can provide knowledge and valuable experience for recovering future animals.

Crunch Time

Even if you properly choose when and where to shoot, you're only halfway to success. It's easy to do everything correctly up to crunch time, then mentally fall apart when shooting. I still struggle, at times, when it comes to the moment of truth. The key is controlling emotions. On the other hand, if I ever reach a point when I no longer get excited when shooting at game, I'll quit. So you need to find a happy medium. Here are a few tips that have either helped or hindered me.

Positives

Early on, I shot at every legal big-game animal that presented a good shot opportunity. By shooting does, small bucks and "non-trophy" animals, I gained valuable experience and confidence. Any newcomer holding out for a "trophy" is dramatically reducing his or her chance of success when an opportunity presents itself. In my opinion, you have to successfully harvest numerous big-game animals with archery tackle before you can expect to maintain composure on a record-class buck.

Shooting confidence plays a large role in success, too. If you think, "Maybe I can make the shot," you're likely to fail. You must believe you will make the shot. Dedicated practice and past success are critical components to rely on.

In practice, I draw and shoot every arrow in slow motion. That way, deliberate motion is second nature at crunch time. Furthermore, I mentally coach myself during the shot. "Wait, wait, okay, nice and slow, pick a spot, aim, aim, aim," is a typical litany for me. You also should have mental coaching plan in mind beforehand.

Negatives

Here are some things that have hindered me from maintaining control at crunch time: One, if an

Trevor Lauber pulls his broadhead-tipped arrows from a practice sandpit as Randy Stock watches.

animal has detected my presence, I tend to panic more than when an animal is totally unaware of me.

Two, on really skittish game like whitetails, pronghorns and turkeys, I have to be really patient with the shot selection so as not to blow the chance.

Three, feeling pressed for time, like on a short hunt, I can become anxious.

Four, I get anxious on long, fruitless hunts, too.

Finally, big antlers have, at times, caused me to fall apart. For this, I concentrate on the animal's eyes until drawing and then switch to an aiming spot behind the shoulder.

Remember, no one always makes the right choices when it comes to the moment of truth. However, you must honestly evaluate your errors and turn them into positive lessons. As for success, let it fuel the confidence fire but don't let it burn out of control either. At crunch time, arrogance and over-confidence can defeat you as quickly as doubt.

Conclusion

When it comes to the moment of truth, you should ooze with confidence because all the equipment choices, tackle setup, practice and preparation have been attended to with due diligence—long before the hunt. Shot placement via accurate shooting is priority one; everything else goes way down the totem pole of importance.

Remember, keep your equipment simple and set it up to be forgiving. Be safe and legal. Encourage youngsters and newcomers to bowhunt. Be supportive and thoughtful of others' equipment choices.

And, most of all, have fun!

BASEMENT BOW SHOP

The tools and techniques needed to set up, maintain and repair the accurate hunting bow are both expensive and extensive. There's no getting around it. You must either rely on and pay for quality bow work from a knowledgeable person at an archery pro shop dedicated to customer service or do it yourself. I use both options. When lack of time dictates, I turn my bow needs over to a proven and trusted bow mechanic. When time is not an issue, I do bow work in my basement bow shop.

The hours I've invested in setting up and maintaining archery tackle at home have also served me well on many remote bowhunts. There's nothing more frustrating than having archery equipment problems occur during those precious few hours of pre-rut when you'd rather be on stand or, worse, during an expensive backcountry hunt. If you do not know how to correct the aliment, it could dramatically delay or ruin the hunt. For these reasons it's paramount to become educated in bow repair and the tools of the trade.

It may take years and several thousand dollars to acquire all the tools and supplies necessary to properly set up, effectively maintain and correctly repair archery tackle. The best advice I have is to buy what you can initially and then acquire additional gear as needs arise. Here is a segregated and prioritized list of bow repair tools and many of the bow repair techniques you should learn to become a self-sufficient bow mechanic.

Primary Tools

- Allen wrench set (most bows and accessories use Allen/hex head bolts and screws)
- Broadhead wrench (for safely tightening and removing broadheads)
- Bow square (to measure nock set height and other bow settings)
- Paper tuning frame (bow tuning)
- Bow press (either portable or full-size to change or twist up string/bus cable, install peep, change limb, cam, etc.)
- Butane torch (to heat insert glue, burn D-loop ends, singe knot ends, etc.)
- Leather bootlace (wrap around string to move tied-in peep or D-loop)
- Fletching jig
- Serving jig (device to effectively re-serve bowstring)
- Arrow cut-off saw
- Electronic grain scale (measures arrow components in grain weight)

Optional Tools

- Nock wrench (for twisting nock within arrow shaft)
- Scissors
- Felt-tip marker pen
- Lighter
- Tap and die set
- Bow draw-weight scale
- Files
- Center punch and mallet (for removing axles)
- Arrow squaring device (ensures a true 90-degree end on arrows and inserts)
- Arrow-length indicator

- Wire cleaning brush (roughens inside of arrow shaft for better insert adhesion)
- E-clip tool (makes removing and installing axle e-clips easy)
- Nock pliers (only if you use brass nock sets)
- Arrow straightener (for aluminum arrows only)
- Broadhead sharpener

Advanced Tools

- Spot-Hogg laser tool (checks for wheel lean)
- Bow vise (holds bow to keep hands free while installing or repairing accessories and to level bow sight)
- Bow level (works in conjunction with the vise to ensure bow and sight are equally plumb)
- Chronograph (measures arrow speed)
- Arrow spine deflection tester (measures static spine)
- Shooting machine (invaluable for arrow tuning and troubleshooting bow problems)

Replacement Parts

- String and bus cable
- Arrow rest launcher arm
- Arrow inserts
- Nocks
- Peep
- Peep tubing
- Bow limbs
- Limbsavers or String Leeches (rubber devices that wear out due to vibration)
- Supplies
- String wax
- Braided #2 nylon serving thread
- String D-loop material
- Insert glue
- Fletch glue
- E-clips
- Adhesive-backed fleece
- Lubricant
- Alcohol or acetone
- Fletches
- Brass nock sets
- Cotton swabs
- Rags

Techniques

- Paper and/or bare-shaft tuning
- Tying a string D-loop
- Re-serving a string
- Tying a finishing knot for serving
- Tying overhand knots
- Reducing wheel lean
- Checking and adjusting wheel timing
- Replacing string and bus cable
- Replacing limbs
- Repairing stripped or damaged threads with a tap and die.
- Fletching arrows

KINETIC ENERGY CHART
Arrow Weight (in grains)

Arrow Speed (feet per second)	300	325	350	375	400	425	450	475	500	525	550	575	600	625	650
180	21.6	23.4	25.2	27.0	28.8	30.6	32.4	34.2	36.0	37.8	39.6	41.4	43.2	45.0	46.8
185	22.8	24.7	26.6	28.5	30.4	32.3	34.2	36.1	38.0	39.9	41.8	43.7	45.6	47.5	49.4
190	24.1	26.1	28.1	30.1	32.1	34.1	36.1	38.1	40.1	42.1	44.1	46.1	48.1	50.1	52.1
195	25.3	27.4	29.6	31.7	33.8	35.9	38.0	401.0	42.2	44.3	46.5	48.6	50.7	52.8	64.9
200	26.7	28.9	31.1	33.3	35.5	37.8	40.0	42.2	44.4	46.6	48.9	51.1	53.3	55.5	57.7
205	28.0	30.3	32.7	35.0	37.3	39.7	42.0	44.3	46.7	49.0	51.3	53.7	56.0	58.3	60.7
210	29.4	31.8	34.3	36.7	39.2	41.6	44.1	46.5	49.0	51.4	53.9	56.3	58.8	61.2	63.7
215	30.8	33.4	35.9	38.5	41.1	43.6	46.2	48.8	51.3	53.9	56.5	59.0	61.6	64.1	66.7
220	32.2	34.9	37.6	40.3	43.0	45.7	48.4	51.1	53.7	56.4	59.1	61.8	64.5	67.2	69.9
225	33.7	36.5	39.4	42.2	45.0	47.8	50.6	53.4	56.2	59.0	61.8	64.7	67.5	70.3	73.1
230	35.2	38.2	41.1	44.1	47.0	49.9	52.9	55.8	58.7	61.7	64.6	67.6	70.5	73.4	76.4
235	36.8	39.9	42.9	46.0	49.1	52.1	55.2	58.3	61.3	64.4	67.5	70.5	73.6	76.7	79.7
240	38.4	41.6	44.8	48.0	51.2	54.4	57.6	60.8	64.0	67.2	70.4	73.6	76.8	80.0	83.1
245	40.0	43.3	46.7	50.0	53.3	56.7	60.0	63.3	66.7	70.0	73.3	76.7	80.0	83.3	86.7
250	41.6	45.1	48.6	52.1	55.5	59.0	62.5	66.0	69.4	72.9	76.3	79.8	83.3	86.8	90.2
255	43.3	46.9	50.5	54.2	57.8	61.4	65.0	68.6	72.2	75.8	79.4	83.0	86.7	90.3	93.9
260	45.0	48.8	52.5	56.3	60.1	63.8	67.6	71.3	75.1	78.8	82.6	86.3	90.1	93.8	97.6
265	46.8	50.7	54.6	58.5	62.4	66.3	70.2	74.1	78.0	81.9	85.8	89.7	93.6	97.5	101.4
270	48.6	52.6	56.7	60.7	64.8	68.8	72.9	76.9	81.0	85.0	89.1	93.1	97.1	101.2	105.2
275	50.4	54.6	58.8	63.0	67.2	71.4	75.6	79.8	84.0	88.2	92.4	96.6	100.8	105.0	109.2
280	52.2	56.6	60.9	65.3	69.7	74.0	78.4	82.7	87.1	91.4	95.8	100.1	104.5	108.8	113.2
285	54.1	58.6	63.1	67.7	72.2	76.7	81.2	85.7	90.2	94.7	99.2	103.7	108.2	112.8	117.3
290	56.0	60.7	65.4	70.0	74.7	79.4	84.1	88.7	93.4	98.1	102.7	107.4	112.1	116.7	121.4
295	58.0	62.8	67.6	72.5	77.3	82.1	87.0	91.8	96.6	101.5	106.3	111.1	116.0	120.8	125.6
300	60.0	65.0	70.0	75.0	80.0	85.0	90.0	94.9	99.9	104.9	109.9	114.9	119.9	124.9	129.9
305	62.0	67.1	72.3	77.5	82.6	87.8	93.0	98.1	103.3	108.5	113.6	118.8	124.0	129.1	134.3
310	64.0	69.4	74.7	80.0	85.4	90.7	96.0	101.4	106.7	112.1	117.4	122.7	128.1	133.4	138.7
315	66.1	71.6	77.1	82.6	88.2	93.7	99.2	104.7	110.2	115.7	121.2	126.7	132.2	137.7	143.2
320	68.2	73.9	79.6	85.3	91.0	96.7	102.3	108.0	113.7	119.4	125.1	130.8	136.5	142.1	147.8
325	70.4	76.2	82.1	88.0	93.8	99.7	105.6	111.4	117.3	123.2	129.0	134.9	140.8	146.6	152.5

FITNESS FOR THE ARCHER

Being physically fit in an archery sense will help you relax, aim steadier and have more confidence for accrate shooting.

Here are some archery-specific exercises:

Three-Way Shoulder Lift

This multi-part exercise targets those muscles used in drawing and holding a bow at full draw.

- Using two dumbbells (start with 4 to 5 pounds/1.8 to 2.25 kg on each side), stand with back straight and knees slightly bent.
- Forward lift, holding a dumbbell in each hand, knuckles facing the wall in front of you.
- Raise both arms simultaneously to just above shoulder height (similar to tossing a horseshoe). Hold for a few seconds, lower the dumbbells slowly to your sides.
- Do 8 to 10 reps.

Next is the lateral lift part of the exercise:

- With the same body form, except with knuckles facing to the side, raise your arms (like flapping wings) to just above shoulder height. Hold.
- Slowly lower dumbbells to your sides.
- Do 8 to 10 reps.

Immediately following these two maneuvers, do a dumbbell military press:

- Raise the weights, knuckles facing backward, so your shoulders and elbows are parallel to the ground; your forearms and hands will be pointing toward the ceiling.
- Raise the weights over your head and touch the dumbbell bars together.
- Do 8 to 10 reps.

Scapular Retraction and Protraction

This move is difficult to isolate at first but once you get the hang of it, it'll help with strength and flexibility in those muscles used when shooting with back tension or a surprise release.

- Stand with hands placed against a wall.
- Pretend you're doing vertical push-ups except keep your arms straight.
- Flex only your shoulder blades in toward each other as if you're trying to hold an apple.
- Arch your back to gain as much space between your scapulas as possible.
- Do 10 to 15 reps.

At the Gym

Rowing machines and latissimus dorsi pull-down machines are excellent. You don't have to do all of these exercises every day. Try splitting them up and trading off on alternate days. Performing these drills consistently will enable you to draw more weight, relax more at full draw, aim steadier and release the arrow with more confidence.

Index

A

Accessories, 12, 29–33, 38
Accuracy, 9, 11, 25, 27, 46, 49, 78, 96–101
Aim, 40, 45, 48
    Gap shooting, 41
    Gun barreling, 41
    Instinctive shooting, 8, 40
Alaska Bowhunting Supply, 37
Allington, Gordon, 72
Aluminum arrow, 19, 20, 21, 22, 37, 38, 76, 80, 81, 101
Anchor, 9, 30, 39, 41, 45, 48, 52, 54, 55, 56
Angle, 74, 75, 113–114, 122
APA Archery, 16
Arm guard, 38, 39, 72
Arrow building, 76–81
Arrow release, 9, 50–57
Arrows, 9, 12, 18–23, 25, 33, 37, 82

B

B-50 Dacron, 36, 37
Bare-shaft tuning, 84, 89
Barrie Archery, 26, 28
Bassham, Lanny, 111
Beman USA, 8, 19, 20
Bitzenburger Machine & Tool, Inc., 77
Black Gold Precision Bowsights, 8
Black Widow Custom Bows, Inc., 35, 38, 51
Bows, 6–13
Bowstrings, 9, 12, 4–17, 36
BowTech, 8
Brace height, 7, 11, 12, 40, 100, 101
Broadheads, 12, 17, 19, 20, 21, 22, 23, 24–28, 33, 38, 53, 57, 63, 64, 72, 78, 79, 80, 82, 83, 84, 91, 100, 101, 115, 117, 122
Brownell, 16
Buck fever, 107
Bushnell Performance Optics, 69

C

Cable, 16, 84, 87, 117
Cam, 11, 17, 84–85, 100, 101, 117
Carbon arrow, 19, 20, 21, 37, 38, 76, 77, 78, 81, 99, 100
Carbon Tech, 77

Carter Enterprises, 55
Cat Quiver, 38
Compound bow, 7, 8, 10, 11, 35, 38, 60
Conditions, 23, 72, 112–117
    Awkward positions, 46, 115
    Rain, 116
    Side slopes, 115
    Snow, 117
    Steep angles, 74, 75, 113–114, 122
    Wind, 115–116, 121
Cowgill, Jim, 89
Cox, South, 10, 12, 53, 66, 97–98, 113
Creep, 15, 16
Cut area, 27–28, 38

D

Dillon Precision Products, Inc., 26, 77
Distance estimation, 66–70, 94
D-loop, 15, 17, 32, 54, 55, 85, 89, 100
Dominant eye, 41, 42
Double Bull Archery, Inc., 69
Draw length, 7, 9, 11, 17, 20, 35, 47, 72, 84, 100
Draw weight, 7, 10, 12, 20, 35, 36, 37, 39, 47, 52, 54, 72, 83, 84, 90, 100
Dynabow, 106

E

Eastman Outfitters, 28
Easton, 19, 20, 22, 37, 76, 77, 89
Eckles, Rich, 66, 117
Eckles, Rob, 66
Eichler, Fred, 35–36, 39
Etherington, David, 36, 38

F

Fast Flight, 17, 36
Feather, 19, 20, 22, 23, 38, 40, 101, 116
Field tip, 64, 80, 87, 91
Finger shooting, 16, 30, 38, 39, 44, 45, 46, 50–52, 83, 85, 101
Fletching, 12, 19, 20, 22, 23, 30, 32, 38, 40, 44, 77, 79, 80, 82,

87, 89, 100, 101, 115, 116
Follow-through, 46, 53, 57, 60, 63
Front-of-center (FOC), 19, 20, 21, 23, 79, 80, 100, 116
Fryman, Travis, 35
Full Draw Outfitters, 106

G

G5 Outdoors, 27, 28, 77
Gap shooting, 41
GlenDel target, 25, 74
Glove, 38, 51
Gold Tip, Inc., 20, 77, 81
Golden Key Futura, 8
Grizzlystick, 38
Gun barreling, 41

H

Handle, 11, 16
Helical, 22, 100
Hicks Archery Products, 59
Hunt, Sam, 74

I

Insert, 22, 26, 38, 80, 87
Instinctive shooting, 8, 40

J

Jirik, Frank, 62
Johnson, Dave, 56
Johnson, Josh, 81
Jones, Josh, 9, 52, 55, 82, 97

K

Kinetic energy, 10, 22, 72, 98, 100, 101
Kirkpatrick, Jim, 95

L

Land, Mark, 35, 38
Lauber, Jessica, 9
Lauber, Trevor, 123
Lauber, Tyler, 8
Length, 11, 19, 21
Let-off, 8, 10, 100
Level, bubble, 30, 115
Limb, 12, 15, 16, 33, 37, 72, 73, 84

Lincoln, Phil, 75
Line shooting, 89
Loesch Enterprises, 59
Longbow, 7, 8, 35, 41

M

Magnus Archery Company, 28
Mathews, Correy, 71
Mathews Archery, 15, 16, 83
McKenzie Sports Products, Inc., 74
McKinley, Dan, 68
Miller, Sam, 7, 25, 77
Montana Black Gold, 8
Morehead, Bill, 5, 41
Muzzy Products Corp., 28, 38

N

National Bowhunter Education Foundation, 122
New Archery Products, 28
Nock, 11, 15, 17, 19, 20, 30, 39, 44, 77, 78, 79, 81, 83, 85, 88, 89, 91, 100
Noise, 15, 23, 27, 33, 38, 39, 72, 75, 81, 88, 98, 100, 101

P

Pape, Josh, 69
Paper testing, 84, 86–88, 89
Paradox, 20
Peep, 16, 17, 31, 32, 43, 47, 48, 49, 117
Pellerite, Bernie, 109
Penetration, 9, 20, 26, 27, 37, 72, 82, 99, 122
Pins, 31, 48, 49, 64, 68
Pope and Young, 7, 19, 67, 106, 108, 110, 114, 117, 121, 123
Posekany, Jim, 19
Position, 46, 115
Powder test, 85, 87
Practice, 8, 41, 46, 63, 64, 93
Preseason preparation, 62–65

Q

Quality Archery Designs, 17
Quiver, 12, 29, 32–33, 38, 39, 117

R

R.S. Bow-Vice, Inc., 115
Ram Products, 77
Range, 74, 92–95, 106
Range finder, 10, 67, 68, 69, 93, 94, 98
Recurve bow, 7, 8, 35, 41
Release, mechanical 8, 9, 17, 30, 44, 45, 46, 53–57, 83, 88, 89, 100, 101, 117
Rest, 12, 30, 44, 46, 53, 84, 85, 87, 88, 90, 91, 101, 117
Riser, 12, 33, 36, 38, 40, 60, 90
Rocket Aeroheads, 28
Rock-It Outdoors, 17

S

Saunders Archery, 51
Serving, 15, 17, 85
Shaft, 12, 19, 20, 21, 22, 23, 26, 33, 37, 44, 77, 81, 100, 117
Shokte broadhead, 38
Shooting form, 7, 9, 39, 42–49, 63
Shrewd Archery Products, 59
Sight, 12, 31, 43, 89, 115, 117
    Fiber optics, 31
    Peep, 16, 17, 31, 32, 43, 47, 48, 49, 117
    Pins, 31, 48, 49, 64, 68
Sight picture, 10, 48
Sims Vibration Laboratory, 8, 32, 33, 38, 39
Slope, 115
Snap-shooting, 8, 39
Sonoran Bowhunting Products, 28
Speed, 9, 10, 11, 12, 15, 16, 17, 23, 36, 96–101, 116
Spine, 19, 20, 21, 36, 40, 78, 79, 81, 83, 84, 86, 87, 88, 90
Spokane Valley Archery, 9, 82
Spot-Hogg Archery Products, 56, 60, 81
Stabilizer, 12, 61
Steel Force (Ballistic Archery, Inc.), 28
Stock, Randy, 123
Strawberry Wilderness Archery Products, 8

Stretch, 15

T

3-D shooting, 23, 68, 71–75, 93, 115, 121
Tab, 9, 38, 51, 59
Target, 25, 26, 41, 46, 74, 75
Target panic, 107
Teflon tape, 59
Thompson, Jerry, 78, 79
Torque, 17, 58–61
Traditional archery, 34–39
Trajectory, 10, 21, 68, 78, 94, 98, 100, 113, 116
True Flight Arrow Company, 76
Tru-Fire Corp., 55
Tuning, 39, 63, 82–91

U

Ulmer, Randy, 48, 123

V

Vane, 19, 20, 22, 23, 38, 79, 100, 116
Velocity, 16, 20, 22, 23, 97, 100, 114
Vibration-dampening device, 12, 30, 33, 39, 40

W

WASP Archery Products, Inc., 28
Weight, 12, 19, 21
Wheel, 11, 16, 17, 44, 84–85, 89
Wickens, Todd, 28
Williamson, Harry, 19, 42, 47, 52
Winner's Choice Custom Bowstrings, Inc., 15, 16
Wood arrow, 21, 38

Y

Yardage estimation, 66–70, 72, 94, 98

Z

Zwicky Archery, Inc., 28

Creative Publishing international
is your complete source of How-to information for the Outdoors.

Available Outdoor Titles:

Hunting Books
- Advanced Turkey Hunting
- Advanced Whitetail Hunting
- Bowhunting Equipment & Skills
- The Complete Guide to Hunting
- Dog Training
- Duck Hunting
- Elk Hunting
- Hunting Record-Book Bucks
- Mule Deer Hunting
- Muzzleloading
- Pronghorn Hunting
- Whitetail Hunting
- Whitetail Techniques & Tactics
- Wild Turkey

Fishing Books
- Advanced Bass Fishing
- The Art of Freshwater Fishing
- The Complete Guide to Freshwater Fishing
- Fishing for Catfish

- Fishing Rivers & Streams
- Fishing Tips & Tricks
- Fishing with Artificial Lures
- Inshore Salt Water Fishing
- Kids Gone Fishin'
- Largemouth Bass
- Live Bait Fishing
- Modern Methods of Ice Fishing
- Northern Pike & Muskie
- Offshore Salt Water Fishing
- Panfish
- Salt Water Fishing Tactics
- Smallmouth Bass
- Striped Bass Fishing: Salt Water Strategies
- Successful Walleye Fishing
- Trout

Fly Fishing Books
- The Art of Fly Tying
- The Art of Fly Tying – CD ROM
- Fishing Dry Flies – Surface Presentations for Trout in Streams

- Fishing Nymphs, Wet Flies & Streamers – Subsurface Techniques for Trout in Streams
- Fly-Fishing Equipment & Skills
- Fly Fishing for Beginners
- Fly Fishing for Trout in Streams
- Fly-Tying Techniques & Patterns

Cookbooks
- America's Favorite Fish Recipes
- America's Favorite Wild Game Recipes
- Babe & Kris Winkleman's Great Fish & Game Recipes
- Backyard Grilling
- Cooking Wild in Kate's Camp
- Cooking Wild in Kate's Kitchen
- Dressing & Cooking Wild Game
- Game Bird Cookery
- The New Cleaning & Cooking Fish
- Preparing Fish & Wild Game
- The Saltwater Cookbook
- Venison Cookery

To purchase these or other Creative Publishing international titles,
contact your local bookseller, or visit our website at
www.creativepub.com

The Complete
FLY FISHERMAN™